Open
Admissions
and the
ACADEMIC LIBRARY

Patricia Senn Breivik

AMERICAN LIBRARY ASSOCIATION

Chicago, 1977

Library of Congress Cataloging in Publication Data

Breivik, Patricia Senn.
    Open admissions and the academic library.

    Bibliography: p.
    1.   Libraries, University and college.
2.   College students—Library orientation.
3.   Socially handicapped—Education (Higher)
4.   Libraries and education.   I.   Title.
Z675.U5B82   027.7   77-5816
ISBN 0-8389-3195-2

Printed in the United States of America

This book would not have been possible
without the help and support of numerous people both at the
COLUMBIA UNIVERSITY SCHOOL OF LIBRARY SERVICE
and at
BROOKLYN COLLEGE
Bernice Martin, Joan Larkin, and Thomas Friedmann
in particular.
It is dedicated to the students in Pratt Institute's
Educating Library Users Class, to those who participated in
the 1972 experiment, with every good wish
for their future, and to a prospective
college student,

Kenneth.

Contents

Foreword

Nothing should be more precious to a nation than its people. Progress, prosperity, and pride come from human resources and not from material resources. It is indeed the educated, skilled, and proud men and women who discover, cultivate, and fully develop all material resources no matter how scarce they are.

No individual is the sole master of his or her destiny and completely responsible for the formation of his or her mind, imagination, wishes, hopes, dreams. One's environment plays a crucial role. The society is certainly responsible for the makeup of one's being and one's actions.

The unfortunate, the disadvantaged, the uneducated, the unskilled have as much right to richness and quality of life as the most fortunate. An individual's taste and desire for pleasure, for comforts, for richness, for success are never less than the taste and desire of the most advantaged. A society founded on decency, compassion, and humanity owes to each of its members the same chance, the same dream.

The open admissions opportunity to a university education takes its roots from this concept. If it is only a temporary tranquilizer for a tenseness; if it is to ease the pain of a restless society; if it is a desperate move to quickly hide the failure of high school education; if it is a tool for politicians to show their superficial care; if the university admission, free for all, is a one-time action and the responsibility ends at that, I tremble for the future of that society.

This book presents and discusses the responsibilities of educators, librarians in particular, in facing the diversity of problems the student encounters once he or she is freely admitted to a university environment. Problems and limitations are not few. To take the consequences of free admissions lightly is short-sighted, risky, and dangerous. I know of no other book such as this present volume, which is based on actual experimental research and addresses the problem directly.

Patricia Senn Breivik has shown through her work a deep interest in this critical issue and has presented a scholarly skill of high order to deal with it. The author during her professional studies both at Pratt and at Columbia demonstrated concern for the role of the librarian in "library instruction" and for the major part that he or she can play in the era of open admissions. This concern has grown throughout her professional career, first as a school librarian, then as a college librarian, and as a member of the faculty and assistant dean at Pratt Institute's Graduate School of Library and Information Science.

As one who has observed Dr. Breivik's growth from the beginning of her studies in librarianship and has witnessed almost her entire professional career, I feel extremely proud, and I wish to congratulate her for this excellent and unique contribution to our literature. I hope this work will be read widely and will be taken seriously. The quality of our university education in an era of open admissions depends on the sincere understanding of the problems which we are now facing and which will not leave us for a long time to come.

NASSER SHARIFY, Dean
Graduate School of Library and Information Science
Pratt Institute
Brooklyn, New York

Introduction

This book is about an educational concept which has become a national commitment: that every student shall have the right to an equable opportunity for higher education. The implementation of this concept is usually referred to as open admissions. At present, "open admissions" has the connotation of postsecondary education for the educationally disadvantaged, and as such it is here to stay, despite changes in birthrates, budget cutbacks, fanfare or no fanfare. It is here to stay for three primary reasons:

1. The academic achievement of American school children is decreasing rather than increasing. After thirteen years of declining scores, the 1975 Scholastic Aptitude Tests (SATs) showed the sharpest drop to date in average scores on both the verbal and mathematics tests.

2. The American economy requires a better-educated citizenry. The U.S. Department of Labor's *Occupational Outlook Quarterly* (Summer 1974) states:

   Nearly a quarter of all job openings between 1972 and 1985 are expected to be filled by persons who will have completed four years or more of college [from 1959 to 1972, only 18% of the jobs were so filled] . . . college graduates will be needed for almost one-third of all white-collar job openings, especially in the professional and technical [3 of 4 openings will require a college degree] and managerial and administrative [1 of 2 openings will require a college degree fields].[1]

The *Occupational Outlook Handbook* for 1974–75 states:

". . . employment growth generally will be fastest in those occupations requiring the most education and training."[2]

Indeed, March 1975 employment statistics showed that although 415,000 college graduates were unemployed, they were the smallest percentage of the 8.4 million jobless when ranked by educational attainment.

3. In a time of international competition, no country can afford to squander its resources—particularly its human resources. The New Careerist movement of the sixties, which was directed at providing employment plus educational experiences to the heretofore hard-core unemployable, gave proof that many educationally disadvantaged adults could, with proper support, perform "with considerable academic success."[3] New York State's 1965 Title I, Higher Education Act, projects showed that "with careful screening, at least 75 percent of those without [even] the high school diploma or its equivalent are able to complete successfully post-secondary credit-bearing offerings."[4]

The story is the same time and time again: even when elementary and secondary schools have failed, with proper support men and women can complete academic work and gain access to employment opportunities for the betterment of their lives and the enrichment of society.

The national commitment to universal higher education, in short, is one of survival.

Given, then, the importance and necessity of open admissions, it is the author's contention that academic administrators, faculty, librarians, and students must step back from the educational process and reevaluate the elements in the educational goal before us. We must rethink long-cherished beliefs and practices.

It is this author's further contention that realistic appraisal of the situation can leave no doubt that the academic library and those involved in it must drastically restructure their priorities and assume a much larger responsibility in the educational process. To do anything less would be to cheat the students of the very promise open admissions offers them. If this is true, we must also face up to the fact that either through mental or physical laziness we have for many years failed to provide all students the only type of education upon which a democracy can flourish.

Although this book is not a scholarly treatise, it has a foundation in research. This research, a controlled experiment at Brooklyn College in 1972, was structured to measure the value of library-based instruction in the learning experiences of the educationally disadvantaged. Methodical research that measures the effects of the library in educational institutions is sparse, and in the area covered by this book, almost nonexistent. The findings from the Brooklyn College experiment proved that it is possible to measure such effects and set the direction for further experimentation that, it is hoped, will add more weight to the findings reported.

Most of the background information and illustrative material focus on the state of New York, not because it is the "only" state or represents some sort of norm, but because it was the framework within which the experiment was conducted.

When American public school systems meet the learning needs of each student, universal access to higher education may lose its remedial connotation, but open admissions will still exist as the right of every individual to an equable opportunity to higher education. It is hoped that this book and the people who read it will play a part in bringing that day closer.

An inescapable responsibility of a democracy
is the unceasing cultivation
of the individual talents and capabilities—
all the abilities of all its people.
To that ideal of promoting individual development
is today added an unusually pressing need for
all the ability the nation can muster.

EDUCATION POLICIES COMMISSION,
NATIONAL EDUCATION ASSOCIATION,
Manpower and Education, p. 7.

CHAPTER ONE

The American Educational System : A Failure

To comment on the failure of the American educational system, one must either be extremely brief or write a book on that topic alone. I shall be brief, for anyone who visits a fairly large public library can pick and choose among books about the deficiencies of schools in the inner city, books describing the failure of schools to deal with the underachievers and the overachievers, books concerned with the shortcomings of elementary schools, high schools, and colleges.

The most glaring failure, of course, is in the inner cities, with their heavy minority populations. The widely publicized *Coleman Report,* published in 1969, documented the fact that education in the United States "remains largely unequal in most regions of the country, including all those where Negroes form any significant proportion of the population."[1] Statistics vary from state to state, but a 1970 New York State sampling of persons 14 years of age and over supports this conclusion. The study, conducted by the Bureau of Post-Secondary Continuing Education of the State Education Department, found that the median for school years completed by white students was 12.1 and fell to 10.8 for black students and 9.1 for Puerto Rican students.[2] With 15,604,415 of New York State's 18,236,951 residents living in urban areas,[3] it is no wonder that the greatest problems and worst failures of the educational system are found in its cities.

Inequities in the funding of education exacerbates this situation. In the larger cities, where there are more learning, discipline, health, truancy, and vandalism problems, the low expenditure per student is another reality of

1

life because of the low economic tax base and because monies to schools often are based on attendance rather than enrollment. The thirty-seven largest cities have less to spend per pupil.[4] Across the country, funding per student in elementary and secondary schools varies from less than $1,000 to over $3,000.[5]

Numerous court cases, state legislative bills, and study commissions have advocated reform of school financing, but nothing has shown any real promise of succeeding.[6] Attempts in four states in the early seventies clearly indicated that equal financing of schools will not come by way of popular demand and the ballot box, for affluent areas, where voting tends to be high, oppose redistribution of funds—as might be expected.[7] Moreover, any strictly even-handed leveling of school spending (the approach that tends to be favored) may reduce the money spent on poorer school children who live in the big urban areas where provision must be made for bilingual classes, higher teaching salaries, and the like.[8] And so the inequities of the American educational system are perpetuated, and the system itself when judged by the academic performance of many high school graduates—not to mention the students who don't graduate—should receive a failing grade.

Indeed, the whole issue of open admissions and the inherent problems in its implementation are major indicators of the failure of the American education system. New York City's dire financial situation in the autumn of 1975 elicited a suggested modification of the City University of New York's (CUNY) open admissions policy so as to require an *eighth* grade reading and mathematics level of high school graduates who sought admission to one of its units.[9] Why are so many graduates of our high schools so totally unprepared for higher education? Why can't they read well or manage basic mathematical processes? Why don't they have even the most elementary skills in information handling?

The basic reasons are fairly clear in the literature, and lie both in content and methodology. Most students find that their educational experiences bear little or no relationship to their lives, nor does there seem to be flexibility within the system to adapt it to their needs. With real and personal problems of their own, they are asked to deal with hypothetical situations which have no direct application to their experiences or expectations. While questioning their own values and existence, they are asked to accept someone else's opinion of what's good for them. While fighting for survival, they are asked to see the beauty of the classic poets and writers. Is it any wonder that our education system has failed them?

Finally, having failed so often, these students feel that failure is the only "route" open to them. They are helpless before an overwhelming amount of information that they have neither the skills nor the developed mental strength to handle. Dealing with an environment of words, they cannot find in them the ideas and concepts they need. Suspicious of the world which has browbeaten them, they do not have the skills to evaluate the information and options before them. They are truly helpless. Is there any question that the American education system has failed them?

The solution certainly does not lie in accepting the norms of the street as the proper or correct ends of education. Even the popular press points to the dangers inherent in legitimizing students' "natural" communication patterns in the classrooms, rather than using their knowledge and experience as the basis for their mastery of verbal and written communication processes.[10] The former approach is misleading in that it sacrifices the ultimate personal success of students for their immediate gratification. It's a cheap, easy way out for the educator, and certainly is not the answer for the student.

How sad that we know the solution, which only the rich can afford. Works by Jean Piaget, Jerome Bruner, and others have provided new insights into how individuals learn, that is, from the interaction of the child with his or her environment rather than from apprehending information from external forces. This concept has led to acceptance of the premise that all subjects can be taught to any child at any stage of development, which in turn has led to "learner-centered reform" in education. At the heart of this reform is the individualizing of the learning process to meet the needs of each student.

In the individualizing of learning, four major dimensions have been identified by which students differ in relation to each other: rate of learning, life situation, learning style, and goals.

> Two of these dimensions are receiving a great deal of attention today; the other two are just beginning to surface. We know quite a bit about reforming the learning curriculum through self-paced learning modules and about gearing education to the situational needs of . . . nontraditional learners. . . . We do not know as much about gearing instruction to the cognitive style of learners, nor have we done any really serious thinking about reform in the content and goals of the curriculum.[11]

Lamentably, even in the areas that have been explored and understood, little has happened in the schools and colleges of our nation. Little more than lip service has been paid by most institutions to individualizing the learning process, such as multiple approaches to learning, doing away with textbooks in favor of multi-resources, providing independent research opportunities to all students. If schools have done better in responsive scheduling and locating educational offerings, one cannot help but wonder if the prime motivating factor has not been finances rather than a desire for educational advancement.

In the meantime, and ahead of many professional educators, laymen such as Alvin Toffler, in his best seller *Future Shock,* have discerned the only logical goal of today's curricula. Toffler points to the inescapable fact that the only viable objective for schools in a time of ever more rapidly expanding and self-outdating information is to teach students how to learn on their own.[12] It has been predicted that "by 1980 the skills most needed to survive will be those of communication. The management and conceptualization of knowledge will become much more important because the rate of increase in knowledge will be so rapid that concentration on specifics will be futile."[13]

Learning of this type will focus students' efforts on the information process itself. Instead of students' receiving preselected packages of information (e.g., a lecture, textbook, or reading list), they will be required to develop the ability to locate independently the sources of information within their chosen disciplines. Instead of students' being limited to a predetermined structure of topic coverage, they will have to develop skills for evaluating and organizing the information they have chosen from the pool of pertinent information. Moreover, only this type of learning can achieve the corollary goal of the learner-centered curriculum, "to make learning maximally effective—not for the *average* student, but for *each* student,"[14] for it creates the framework within which students can work at their own levels of potential and at their own speed.

Yet how many graduates of teachers' colleges have learned how to learn? How many have had experience in working not from a preselected set of materials but from the total resources available to them, and to such an extent that they are comfortable with such procedures? Relatively few, I am sorry to say. Our cerebral acceptance of the "information explosion" has far to go before filtering into the fiber of our personal and professional lives. Too often one still hears an educated(?) person boast, "I never had to go into the library the whole time I was in college."

In a seminar at Teachers College in New York City I got to know a woman who had taught nursing for several years and who had forward-looking views on the responsibilities for tomorrow's nurses. A very intelligent woman, who took her teaching duties seriously enough to pursue a doctorate, she had never even heard of the *Index Medicus,* one of the major in-print access keys to current information in the medical field, until I mentioned it in discussion. And there was the very library-oriented English professor who, after hearing a lecture on the card catalog to English freshmen, confessed rather sheepishly, "I'm ashamed to admit that I didn't know a lot of that."

This, then, is perhaps the ultimate failure: Educators (with a capital E) have not put into practice what they know, even in the training of their own ranks. Few steps have been taken to ensure that, as part of their formal education, teachers will acquire the knowledge, skills, and motivation which are prerequisite to their own lifelong learning, as well as to their structuring of such learning experiences for their students.

Yet it is from this apex of failure that a new ray of hope has emerged. The overwhelming demands which an effective open admissions policy places upon traditional institutions have driven these institutions to new considerations, new approaches, and a new openness.

CHAPTER TWO

Open Admissions : An Open Door for Students

Over the years, our legislative and judicial leaders have slowly moved this country toward the freedom of opportunity which the Declaration of Independence and the Constitution have prescribed for each citizen. Increasing acceptance of the concept that universal opportunity applies to education beyond the high school has developed over the years, and establishment of the land-grant colleges in the United States was a major step toward open admission policies whereby every high school graduate is guaranteed entrance into college.[1] Civil rights court decisions and legislative efforts have supported the concepts that knowledge has come to be central to society and must be the right of everyone.[2] A major objective of the U.S. Office of Education is to bring equality of educational opportunity to every citizen, and its priority at this juncture is the economically and culturally depressed youth in our large urban centers.[3] Moreover, the national concern for equality of access has been extended to the graduate level.[4]

Open admission considerably preceded its great flurry of publicity at the onset of the seventies. Since 1960, California has guaranteed access to higher education to all of its high school graduates, and many state universities, for all practical purposes, have an open admissions policy. However, it was the City University of New York's switch from elitism to egalitarianism in 1970 that was heralded as "the academic world's most radical response so far to explosive changes in the nation's cities."[5] Implementation of the national commitment to universal higher education was seen not only as the city's responsibility but also as the responsibility of the educators. As

CUNY's vice chancellor for academic affairs wrote: "CUNY's open admissions policy is a good example of an institution taking a clear social position: accepting a public responsibility to serve as poverty interrupter for New York . . . (at stake) is the unity of the City itself. For the University can really change the streets."[6]

The rationale for acceptance of such a gargantuan responsibility was basically moral: the lack of achievement of socially and economically depressed youth was finally acknowledged as more the fault of a poor elementary and secondary educational system than the fault of the students.[7] There was both the broad aim of conserving our nation's human resources and the humanitarian aim of helping the young people,[8] for, in the last analysis, "the chief hope of the low-income nonwhite family is for some improvement in economic status. But the prospect for such an improvement depends on access to education."[9]

It was acknowledgment of the latter, coupled with the very low percentage of nonwhite students enrolled in CUNY in 1969, that created the explosive campus situation that eventually forced the date for CUNY's open admissions policy to be moved forward from 1975 to 1970. At that point it was immediate and practical results, rather than long-range philosophical outcomes, that were sought (i.e., the ethnic balancing of the student body and the preservation of educational facilities and programs). One New York State legislator explained his support in terms of dollars and cents, saying, "It costs $2,000 a year to keep a ghetto kid in jail."[10]

Whatever the reasons—noble or expedient—open admissions had begun, and educators were answering the challenge of responsibility for educational justice, of providing full access and equal educational opportunity for all, rather than relinquishing it to the courts.[11] With this responsibility, however, came several others. Educators now had the obligation to ensure that the lowering of admissions barriers was not another invitation to failure for the disadvantaged—that, at the same time, degree standards would be maintained.[12] This responsibility led to another: the college had to assume responsibility for areas of instruction that were traditionally the high schools',[13] which led to development of remedial or compensatory programs.

Most of these programs were proof of the assumption that writing, reading, listening, and speaking skills are the most acute deficiencies of disadvantaged students and necessitate strong emphasis on the process of learning rather than on conventional subject matter. As a consequence, four basic formats for packaging this type of learning were developed:

1. A remedial group of courses for all students, differentiated from the regular curriculum and providing reading and study skills

2. Regular class attendance, supplemented by tutorial assistance
3. A reduced load of regular courses, with an added component of study-skills labs, special courses, and tutoring
4. A summer preparatory program for skills building, college orientation, and self-confidence building, before regular courses in the fall.[14]

Most colleges use more than one (or even all) of these approaches with open admissions students, for one thing is sure: if there is to be any chance of success, educationally disadvantaged students cannot be treated as lumps of common clay that are to be molded into one form. Thus colleges try many approaches; and many programs, designed to meet the needs of disadvantaged students, have been developed.

Often the work of such programs is channeled through the college department which is responsible for services related to the institution's total open admissions program, and there is no question that at least some of these activities have demonstrated elements of success. The SEEK[15] program, for example, had a dropout rate of roughly 60 percent during its first three years—which is far from discouraging since it was only 10 percent worse than the national rate for college students with more conventional preparation; and in the winter of 1969, when its first four students graduated, two were *cum laude* and all four were headed for graduate school.[16] After less than a decade of operation, the program, which began with 1,000 students, had an enrollment of 10,700 students and more than 1,700 students had graduated.[17] This success is perhaps even more amazing if one considers the administrative problems the SEEK program has endured throughout its existence.[18]

However, the situation is far from bright. As necessary as remedial work is, there is often not enough support for these programs. Many black students and faculty groups have tended to avoid the skill-development issue because they are primarily interested in developing a black consciousness and have directed their efforts toward establishing black studies programs.[19] Then there is the question whether such work should receive academic credit. "Remedial work" used to imply that a student had taken the same work in high school and had done badly, but often this is not the case with graduates of today's ghetto schools; thus it may be fair to give students credit for such work, just as students who begin a new language are given credit despite the fact that the language may also be taught on the high school level.[20] If no credit were given and little importance is placed on remedial work, there is little chance that students will learn the skills that are necessary for their academic success.

Of all the indictments against compensatory education, the one that comes closest to the truth is that such programs ignore the individual and try to assimilate the students, as closely as possible, to the institution's norm for regular students.[21] The reason that is often cited for this tendency is fear that any other aim will result in a dilution of standards.[22] Another reason cited for the lack of evidence that educational programs prompt institutions to make meaningful revisions of their traditional methods, goals, or expectations is that some teachers and administrators are so accustomed to functioning under the old system that they adhere to educational theories that are geared to the traditional student who came to college with adequate academic skills.[23]

This relative lack of change in academic programs is causing repercussions with open admissions students. From the very beginning of their admission to college, they are confronted by all kinds of things that make no sense to them.[24] It is predictable that these students will eventually realize that a major cause of their problems is that the educational system is not designed to accommodate students who come from backgrounds of limited education, and there is every reason to doubt that militant minority students, with a desire to redress well-documented grievances, will be satisfied by an educational program whose end is submission to the traditional norms of the white establishment.[25]

Yet, despite problems and prophecies of doom, open admissions is still a reality in the CUNY system after six years. The key to this may be in the history of the institution itself. For example, City College, which was the site of the 1969 student confrontation that caused the premature launching of CUNY's open admissions policy and which was the senior college most drastically affected by the policy, had evolved through a similar experience; that is, it had been created in 1837 as a Free Academy which would be open to the children of the poor as well as the rich, a very radical notion for its day. In fact, when the plan was proposed, a number of educators and civic leaders doubted whether poor children had any innate capacity for instruction.[26] So it was particularly fitting that CUNY should serve as the stage for implementation of an open admissions policy.

If the foregoing description of the beginning of open admissions within the CUNY system, though mentioning the major criticisms and concerns of its critics, is rather positive, it is so because it reflects the hopes and determination of many students and educators, including myself. Now, approximately six years after the start of open admissions in New York City, supporters and critics of the policy are farther from reconciliation than before it began. Accusations of high attrition and lower standards clash with accusations of failure by the CUNY administration to provide the support to make such a program viable, and financial setbacks are aggravating the situation.

Part of the conflict is due to the statistics on the program, as they are subject to much suspicion and give rise to conflicting interpretations. Much of this was caused by the inadequate and decentralized recordkeeping that was in effect when open admissions began. The most recent published statistics follow the 1970 enrollees through four semesters and constitute a fairly bright report card for open admissions. Compiled under David E. Lavin, associate professor of Herbert H. Lehman College of the City University of New York, who has been associated with several authoritative publications on open admissions, the study concludes:

> When the CUNY net retention data over four semesters are compared with national data, it is apparent that considerably more attrition will have to occur before the CUNY net retention rate approaches the threshold defined by the national data.[27]

Other testimony to the value of the CUNY open admissions policy is the dogged determination of administrators directly involved with the programs to proceed with them despite political pressures and the staggering budget cuts of 1975. For example, President John W. Kneller of Brooklyn College, in the same newspaper interview in which he lamented that budget cuts threatened to reduce the college "to utter mediocrity," stated his conviction that the college should be kept open to the academically underprepared despite the fact that it was, on the average, more expensive to educate them.[28]

CUNY Chancellor Robert J. Kibbee was forced by severe budget cuts to propose a restructuring of the university to cut its operations by 20 percent, including a reduction in student body over a three-year period from 220,000 to 180,000 full-time-equivalent students. He proposed to safeguard open admissions by providing that "all high school graduates from the previous June would be admitted automatically so long as they applied by March 1" and by preserving free tuition, without which an open admissions policy would be meaningless.[29]

Of course, it is impossible to know the actual motivation for such support of open admissions. To be against the policy would invite much antagonism from many quarters of the city. Yet, because of increasing budget pressures, administrators could evince "legitimate" reasons for speaking against continuance of the policy, if in fact they were looking for a politically acceptable out. The fact seems to be that despite administrative and educational problems and the mounting financial problems surrounding implementation of the policy, there have been enough results in terms of student success to elicit the ongoing support of many top administrators.

Of course, not all educators favor universal higher education. The basic controversy over adopting an open admissions policy is between two views of academic institutions' roles: to provide the privilege of higher education to relatively few talented students, with the responsibility of meeting the requirements for graduation and a degree left to the students, or to provide an education for as many students as possible (though, ideally, not at the expense of standards), with the responsibility of recruiting students and helping them live up to its standards left with the college.[30] In the case of CUNY, little recruitment was necessary, but complicated, diverse programs of financial, counseling, and academic support were adopted at considerable expense to the institutions. These programs, though aimed at preparing students for academic success within existing standards, were seen as largely impotent and resource draining by those who opposed the policy.

To be seen in its proper perspective, however, open admissions practices and the subsequent problems cannot be thought of as a separate and unique phenomenon in higher education. Rather, it is a specialized expression of the general trends in higher education of the last decade or so. The complexities of our age require that an increasingly large number of people who have learned to think scientifically will be needed, and the rapidity with which information is produced and outdated requires that these people continue to learn throughout their working lives.[31] Unfortunately, changing learning needs and changing, expanding undergraduate student bodies are finding little response in undergraduate programs. For the most part, colleges seem to be just coping with these changes and, somehow, providing the same kinds of materials and services to more and more students in more and more courses.[32] The trend toward universal higher education simply exacerbates the problem; for by increasing the number of students, the amount of diversity in the students' academic backgrounds and in their socioeconomic levels is also increased.[33]

The final answers to open admissions will be a long time in the making, but it cannot be doubted that this concept has deeply shaken the foundations of the old ivory tower. The subsequent examination of the structure for weaknesses is in itself a major accomplishment, and one that should hold answers for all of public education. Whether the old tower can be strengthened and improved or whether a new structure will ultimately be required, it cannot be doubted that the students—all students—will benefit.

CHAPTER THREE

A
Twentieth-Century
Cop-out ● The Academic
● Library

"If you don't know, ask." Most people live by this adage. When they have a problem or need to know something, they ask the nearest person, perhaps a friend or neighbor. The success or failure of this practice quite obviously depends on the education and experience of one's neighbors and friends. A well-educated person who has recourse to lawyers, doctors, and other professionals can survive very nicely in this manner, but if the person who lives in a disadvantaged community gets an accurate and sufficient reply to a query, it is most likely by sheer chance.

Very few people go to a library for the answers to their questions or problems. In fact, recent studies in Baltimore, Syracuse, and Seattle proved that very few people ever think of the library as a source of information for solving their problems. And it is interesting how little librarians concern themselves with the lack of library use. To be sure, numerous library-use studies have been conducted, beginning with the very fine work of Douglas Waples and Leon Carnovsky, who in the thirties utilized scientific approaches to study readers' uses of libraries and the social implications of reading. Little along this line has been done since then, and most use studies have been one-time assessments of particular libraries that have totally ignored the multitudes of nonusers. Even Waples, in his 1936 study of libraries in academic institutions, was content to refer to an unpublished doctoral study which indicated "that the students withdrawing the most books from the library rank highest in scholarship."[1]

Nowadays many librarians are running scared. Experience has taught them that in times of tight economies they are not able to compete with other agencies and departments for budgetary funds; that, as part of larger bargaining units, they have little or no clout; that their image is miserable; and that, compared with policemen, firemen, garbage collectors, and other public servants, they are the first to be dismissed. In educational institutions, librarians tend to be the first to go—low on the professional totem pole, both in reality and in attitudes, and clearly not in the mainstream of their schools' pursuits. Far beyond pride or blindness, I believe, this precarious position makes it almost impossible for libraries to own up to their superfluousness, as they presently function. Until some in-depth, realistic evaluations can be made and unless realignments of priorities ensue, the basic position of librarians in their communities cannot improve. Even the president of the United States knows that the Library of Congress doesn't require a librarian at its head.

What, then, has been the record of the academic library? A 1970 survey by Patricia Knapp looked into the question of how libraries had responded to trends in higher education.[2] The findings were not encouraging, as the changes were largely superficial, rather than the reappraisal and restructuring of service commitments to meet the changing goals of the libraries' parent institutions. There had been changes in buildings, such as the establishment of undergraduate libraries on university campuses, and decentralization of collections; there had been changes in the collections, to add more nonprint materials and to establish ethnic collections; and there was the standard of the library-college movement, bravely upheld by its small legion, plus a growing concern for independent study. The parallel between the lack of real change in undergraduate curricula and in academic libraries is obvious. Changes in location and additions to collections can only (though often necessary) scratch the surface of the real job at hand, that is, facilitating learning by students.

Academic libraries, one would assume, exist to facilitate the educational goals of their parent institutions, to help students learn how to learn, to make possible the independent study advocated by educators, to help students deal with their problems and live in ways that give life greater meaning, greater effectiveness, and greater satisfaction. It is not enough that informational resources be available, nor even that a student be encouraged to use them. Students must be provided with experiences which convince them that using the library is a necessary and meaningful part of education, and they must be able to function independently and effectively in these pursuits.[3] This requires that students be able to locate, evaluate, and use information. Even the federal government has recognized the need to educate the users of information: the President's Science Advisory Committee recommended in 1963 that schools and colleges develop programs to teach students how to retrieve and use published information.[4] Yet, despite the fact that serious attention has been paid to library instruction in professional literature since the thirties, it is difficult to assess libraries' accomplishment of this educational mission because of lack of research in this area.[5]

The library-use studies do not answer the question—in fact, they almost never address it—of how library use affects school achievement. This omission is difficult to rationalize since no other area of library investigation holds more potential for capturing the attention of students, faculty, and administrators. It is even harder to explain since, as far back as 1932, a positive relationship was determined between reading in the library and scholarship. That early study, conducted by Alvin C. Eurich at the University of Minnesota, found that although there was no perceptible difference in the intelligence ratings of students who read in the library and those who didn't, grade-point averages revealed a definite and statistically significant relationship between library reading and scholarship.

> This fact becomes even more striking in view of a negligible relationship that was secured between the total amount of reading and either intelligence, or scholarship. In other words, the total amount of reading does not appear to aid a student in his scholarship. The distinguishing trait is that he goes to the library to read and study.[6]

While the results of any single study at a particular university cannot be widely generalized, it would seem that further studies would have been conducted by libraries at other institutions in an attempt to substantiate the findings at the University of Minnesota. In fact, however, little has been built on Eurich's foundation in the forty-odd years since he undertook his investigation.

Now, when college survival has gained prominence over qualifying for Phi Beta Kappa keys, the role of library use in the academic success of students must be carefully examined. To date there have been few studies in this area, and those that have been made deserve reexamination and wider publicity. For example, a statistically significant correlation was found between library use and persistence among college freshmen in certain majors at California State Polytechnic College, Pomona;[7] and at Eastern Illinois University a study found a correlation between grade-point average and use of the college library.[8] A particular difficulty in such studies is that grading criteria and teaching methods often do not take account of the type of values normally achieved through library use,[9] so that often, even when students have mastered information-handling skills and regularly utilize library resources, there is no method within traditional classroom evaluation procedures to determine the extent to which such activities are responsible for the academic success of the students.

If the aforementioned findings are valid, there are two immediate implications for academic library programs. First, counseling and orientation toward greater library use need to be fostered, since such use may well be productive of better academic success and persistence. Second, students and faculty have to be made aware of the importance and validity of instruction in how to use the library and its resources, for there can be no doubt that if library use can be correlated to academic success, educated library use may well produce a higher academic achievement.

To achieve this, measurement tools better suited for determining the educational support value of library use and mastery of information skills must be developed. To date, however, this problem has never been adequately dealt with in terms that are meaningful to anyone other than the librarians who are satisfied with pre- and post-tests of library skills. It is all too evident that unless librarians can measure the value of library use and library-based instruction in terms of students' academic success, neither students, faculty, nor administrators will be much interested in the process.

Some professionals feel that the failure of libraries to meet changing needs in higher education is not surprising, since, as was pointed out in chapter 1, our nation's schools and colleges are outmoded and out of step, and libraries, in particular, have never been noted for innovation or radical thrust.[10] But this is an obvious cop-out. The very nature of the problem and the methods already indicated for its solution dictate that libraries must extend help to initiate reform in higher education to a degree never before undertaken.

Beginning with the stated, obvious, and implied goals of their parent institutions, academic libraries must take a leadership role in formulating objectives which maximize the use of information resources (of which they are the most knowledgeable) and clearly indicate to administrators, faculty, and students the relationship of these objectives to their educational goals.[11]

The major problem in academic libraries' taking such a leadership role, interestingly or sadly—depending on one's point of view—is not so much suppression by the faculty or administration as lack of unified commitment on the part of the librarians. Trevor Dupuy, with true insight, describes this ambivalence in his book, *Ferment in College Libraries:*

> It is the aim of the "responsive" librarian to acquire as much as possible of the intellectual output of mankind, and then to organize it so that it is readily accessible. If the clients of the library don't make full

use of this material, once it is so organized, this is their responsibility. The "responsive" librarian assumes that faculty members know all they need to about using a library, and that it is a faculty responsibility to motivate students to use the library.

The "active" librarian is probably just as eager as the "responsive" librarian to collect and organize the intellectual output of mankind. But to him this is only incidental to an aim to make the library a dynamic element in the educational process. He assumes that the faculty does not know all that there is to know about using a library, that they are not fully familiar with the most current literature in their fields, and that the faculty probably needs help in motivating students to make the most effective use of the library.[12]

It could be argued that in the daily functioning of academic libraries such a split would not matter that much, since the two personality types could be assigned responsibilities that match their philosophical convictions. In reality, however, the split produces isolation from the concerns of the rest of the institution which all but precludes assumption of a leadership role by the library, as well as preoccupation with internal politicking that tends to sap much of the library's personnel strength. Indeed, the ultimate result often is not only forfeiting a leadership role on the campus but further erosion of the library's poor or inconsequential image.

If this is the general record of the academic library, let's look at a concrete example. The policy of open admissions, that is, the guaranteed opportunity for every New York City high school graduate to attend college, was first enunciated in the 1964 master plan of the New York City Board of Education. The policy was to go into effect in CUNY in September 1975, but in the spring of 1969 City College was the focal point for black student anger over the imbalance of minority and white students in CUNY, compared to the racial makeup of the city; and on July 9 the Board of Higher Education approved a historic resolution advancing the target date for open admissions from 1975 to September 1970, subject to the provision of sufficient funds by the city and state governments to finance this major move.[13] Though time, money, and space were far from abundant, in autumn of 1970 CUNY admitted 35,000 freshmen—15,000 more than in the previous year.[14]

To any librarian of a romantic or idealistic nature, the opportunity to match one of the greatest challenges to face education with the unknown strength of librarianship in the higher education learning process was exciting; to some of those who worked within CUNY in 1970, the lure was very nearly irresistible. Yet the realities of the situation were far from romantic. During the spring, CUNY libraries, as did other departments, hurried through plans to meet the "invasion." The Open Admissions Committee of Brooklyn College Library, for example, projected four means for meeting the needs of the new students:

1. A division of special service, with its own office, to head up services to academically unprepared students
2. Preparation of a student handbook
3. Preparation of a videotape on use of the card catalog
4. Use of the library newsletter as an agent for educating students in the activities and use of the library.[15]

In the same report the committee stated: "While open admissions is certain to compound existing problems, it can, at the same time, provide an opportunity to reassess our goals, priorities, policies, etc., and our methods of achieving them and provide the necessary staff, facilities, etc., essential to effective service."[16] This philosophy seemed to herald open admissions as the rationale for demanding all the staff, facilities, and funding which the library had been seeking for some time, plus more! How pervasive the tendency was in CUNY libraries to use open admissions as a means for meeting existing needs, that is, as a means to their own ends, is impossible to say. However, a subsequent analysis of CUNY library plans revealed "little correlation (in fact, almost none at all) in the statement of library needs and the projections for the City University in 1971 and then in 1975."[17]

College and library planning should have been helped by the fact that CUNY had been involved in educating disadvantaged students for about five years prior to the beginning of open admissions, through such programs as College Discovery and SEEK, which had been recruiting, counseling, and tutoring such students and providing them with as much as $50 per week as a living stipend.

A survey, sent to CUNY's chief librarians[18] during the November after open admissions began, drew responses from ten of the thirteen CUNY colleges which were in existence before 1970 and which served freshmen-level students. Roughly speaking, the number of entering freshmen tended to double from fall of 1969 to fall of 1970 in these colleges. In one college it more than doubled; in several it increased about a third.

In most instances the libraries were not assigned a significant number of new professional or nonprofessional positions over the year. Two college libraries received no additional professional positions, two received one, three received two, and one received three. One college library received no additional nonprofessional positions, two received two, one received three, two received four, one received five, and one received eight.

It was difficult to draw conclusions as to whether the libraries received additional resources to meet the new demands which open admissions created, as the information was so variously presented. However, three libraries commented that for 1970/71 they had received no additional funds over the previous year, and one had its funds for supplies and binding decreased. Three did not indicate amounts or comment on funding; this could mean that they did not choose to answer this part of the question or that they did not receive additional funds. The only instance where additional space was provided was where buildings had been rented for classes at some distance from the campus and a small reserve and reference section had been established at that location. This same library had been promised additional space on campus, but the promise did not materialize. Thus it could not be seen from additional provisions—where there were additional provisions—that the institutions had acknowledged increased needs for the libraries, even with the significant increase in student enrollment.

Eight librarians felt that the situation created in their libraries by open enrollment was about as difficult as had been anticipated; one thought it less difficult than anticipated; and one commented that there was "no situation"—the libraries were just busier than usual. On a scale of 1 to 10 (1 = completely unprepared, 10 = completely prepared), six librarians gave their libraries a 5 or 6 on preparedness for open enrollment when school began; one each gave their library a 2, a 3, and a 9. One commented that the staff was prepared but that there was seating and space for only a little over a third of the enrollment.

Three libraries did not conduct studies or make plans for open enrollment prior to the fall. Two libraries set up department committees to make such studies and/or recommendations, but little in the way of results seems to have come directly from these committees. One library set up a library skills center, under two full-time professionals. Another made plans for increased public service and freshman orientation. One established a working relationship with the Basic Education Skills Department of its college to prepare lectures for all students in basic-skills courses and to prepare lists of suitable readings.

Several libraries were in contact with the various departments of the colleges and/or SEEK representatives for coordinating mutual responses to open enrollment. In three cases the initiative came from the librarian, in four cases it was a mutual approach, and in one case students contacted the library directly with regard to freshman orientation. Two libraries indicated no involvement in such contact.

In most instances the responsibility for the libraries' planning and providing services to basic-skills students was not assigned but was a "kept" responsibility of the chief librarians. A special services center was established under the responsibility of one of the two assigned professionals. A special services committee was set up at one college by "borrowing" staff as needed from the other divisions. At three colleges, librarians were hired by SEEK or similar offices to work with basic-skills students (at one of these institutions, the librarians so assigned now come under the authority of the chief librarian). One library placed this responsibility on the reference librarian.

Formal instruction of freshmen in the use of library and library materials generally consisted of orientation tours, group lectures in the library, and classroom teaching—without any particular approach seeming to have the edge over the others. Often the library let the faculty know what services were available, and then the initiative rested with the faculty to request such services. Thus the responsibility can be said to have rested on both the librarians and the faculty. One college library was requested to participate regularly in the orientation program, and it made tours available during registration and at the beginning of the semester. Only one library provided formal instruction to every freshman; another indicated "hopefully, yes" to the library survey; the other eight said no. Six libraries provided library handbooks; one made information available through the general handbook and leaflets; the other three said no.

Seven libraries reported that no changes had been made in acquisition policies as a direct result of open enrollment. One did not answer. One had been ordering more remedial material; another had been ordering more high school–level mathematics texts. As one librarian commented, however, "acquisitions policy calls for continuous changes in emphasis as curriculum shifts. . . . Thus, increased purchasing of Black, ethnic, and urban studies began several years ago." Seven libraries had been purchasing nonprint materials on a regular basis. Phonograph recordings were mentioned most frequently, with filmstrips and tapes next. Other items were filmloops, cassettes, videotapes, slides, transparencies, and TV kinescopes. Two libraries indicated that audiovisual materials were not part of the collection at their colleges. One library was ordering nonprint materials with basic-skills students in mind; another was working this out with the Basic Skills Department. The others did not indicate any plans to do so.

Several conclusions could be derived from this survey:

1. The libraries had not been successful in competing with other departments of the colleges for additional positions and provisions in keeping with the increase in student enrollment.
2. In the senior colleges, the chief thrust for meeting the needs of educationally disadvantaged students came from outside the library, and there was, as of then, no trend in ways of meeting the library needs of these students.

3. There seemed to be a lack of appreciation for the education function of the libraries, as only one college asserted that every freshman received formal instruction in the use of the library and its materials.

Not until January 14, 1972, eighteen months after the launching of CUNY's open admissions policy, did the professional organization of CUNY librarians officially support the policy. Their resolution read that the Executive Council of the Library Association of the City University of New York:

1. Calls upon all librarians, in readers' services and technical services alike, to enlarge their efforts in support of the Open Admissions Program through an increased counseling and instructional role.
2. Calls upon the Chief Librarians of the senior and community colleges to undertake further steps practical for implementation of such programs.
3. Appeals to the administrative officers of the CUNY universities and colleges to help these programs by giving all necessary technical and moral support.[19]

As was noted in the general description at the beginning of this chapter, CUNY libraries were far from meeting the initial challenges of open admissions, much less from assuming a leadership role in the transition. Unfortunately, a study of eight publicly supported urban colleges and universities across the United States, which was conducted more than three years after the survey of CUNY libraries, showed little improvement over the situation uncovered by the CUNY study.[20]

CHAPTER FOUR

A Challenge
for Academic Libraries

●

●

Despite the record thus far, our country's commitment to universal higher education must eventually exert added pressure for library-oriented learning. The problem is quite simple: How can colleges and universities with open admissions policies respond to all the young people who present themselves for education when, by the thirteenth grade, the spread in students' academic abilities has stretched to eleven years or more?[1]

To date, government support for research into an effective library response to the needs of disadvantaged persons has for the most part been directed toward public libraries. At a 1964 conference on providing library service to disadvantaged people in New York State in relation to antipoverty programs, attention was given to a project which would "test and demonstrate library skills and techniques effective in bringing this socio-economic group into the library to use its material and services for personal gain and satisfaction."[2] These goals highlight two crucial elements that academic libraries must keep in mind if they are to meet the challenge of open admissions: educationally disadvantaged students must (1) be attracted into the library and (2) be able to experience and thus perceive the library as a direct aid to their personal gain and satisfaction, that is, a direct aid to their academic success.

Of course, lack of financial support usually provides the library with an excuse for copping out. And copping out it is. For if academic libraries had a clear understanding of the nature of the herculean task (i.e., one which all but requires library-oriented learning) facing open admissions administrators and faculty,[3] they would be in a position to start demanding money.

21

The first step in meeting this challenge is much more aggressiveness by libraries in helping their parent institutions, as well as their own departments, redefine their educational goals. The necessary shift from content mastery to lifelong learning and the focus on basic study and communications skills in order to meet the needs of society in general and of disadvantaged students in particular require a more predominant role for libraries. To accomplish these ends it is obvious that it is not enough to stimulate students to use the library; they must be provided with experiences which convince them that using the library is a necessary and meaningful part of education.[4] Furthermore, there is no way to do this unless academic libraries move to the front ranks, with their planning boards.

Since such a shift is not easy, it is fortunate that beneficial side effects generally accrue to the libraries of institutions that have open admissions policies. Usually the increased difficulties in educating disadvantaged students encourage administrators and faculty to set clear learning objectives to facilitate success. Since such objectives must be directed toward the areas cited in the preceding paragraph, a more creative and friendly working relationship frequently seems to develop between remedial skills departments and the library than is usually the case. In the City University of New York, the basic-skills departments at Queens College, City College, and Brooklyn College hired their own librarians to work with their students. (At City College these librarians are now under the jurisdiction of the institution's head librarian.) At Queensborough Community College the library staff of the Basic Skills Department gives lectures to all students who take basic-skills courses and it works with the library staff in preparing lists of suitable readings and in ordering nonprint materials for the students' courses. The list could go on and on.

Libraries which have a clear vision of their educational function, if politically minded, can use their knowledge and the receptive atmosphere to ensure positive curricular and instructional modification throughout the college. The era of the split personality must end, for the new or more aggressive approach by libraries and librarians is the only logical tactic when the function of the college library is seen in the perspective of our national educational needs and goals.

For example, in a study supported by the National Advisory Commission on Libraries and the National Book Committee in 1967, recent major social changes were cited as having produced five principal responsibilities for today's libraries and for shaping the context within which they must operate:

1. To support formal education from prekindergarten through graduate and professional schools

2. To sustain the increasingly complex operations of the Government and the economy of the country
3. To provide opportunities for continuing self-education and retraining
4. To play a role in the reintegration into the society of groups now largely isolated and excluded by their lack in education and training
5. To provide resources (with effective access) for an informed public opinion and for personal cultural and intellectual growth and individuation.[5]

Each of these responsibilities has implications for the functions of college libraries, but they have been preceded by more than forty years of concerned exploration to determine how college libraries could more effectively meet such responsibilities. In 1937 the Association of American Colleges commissioned Harvie Branscomb to investigate how the college library could better be coordinated with a college's educational and recreational programs. This study, financed by the Carnegie Corporation, produced Branscomb's *Teaching with Books,* which could well be considered the birth of the "active" movement in college librarianship.[6] Addressed primarily to college faculty and administrators, this study investigates the library's educational effectiveness and considers the extent to which the efforts of the library are integrated with those of the institution as a whole.

Two other early publications in the "active" movement are Louis Shores's "The Library Arts College, a Possibility in 1954?",[7] his first statement on the library-college concept (which had been delivered at the Chicago Century of Progress Exposition in 1934), and Louis R. Wilson's 1941 paper for the Institute for Administrative Officers of Higher Institutions, "The Use of the Library in Instruction,"[8] in which he explored the forces within and outside the college that had increased the use of the library in college instruction and suggested how library use and instruction might be more effective.

These three position papers are also interesting because they represent two fundamental elements that have usually been lacking in academic libraries' approaches and that are particularly needed today. These papers were basically addressed to academic administrators and teaching faculty, not to librarians. They were "selling" the support value of libraries in achieving the espoused educational goals of the educators—the only sound approach —yet many academic librarians seem too busy defending their shaky "turf" to see themselves as servants. The biblical admonition that "he that is first shall be last and he that is last shall be first" has long been ignored in the struggles for budget and faculty status. Librarians have yet to learn that they can only lose, so long as they strive politically to be equal with the teaching faculty, who always greatly out number them. At the same time, called upon to fulfill their much needed roles in reaching the educational goals of their institutions, academic librarians demur with such familiar statements as: "I can't do research and publish because I have to work at a desk from 9 to 5 and only have one month off in the summer"; or "The library can't meet the current needs of students and faculty, much less offer new services when our budget has been cut and prices have gone up."

The thirties also saw the birth of the library-college movement, the significance of which lies not so much in what it has accomplished (actually, it has achieved remarkably little) as in the fact that it is the only original, theoretical, and thorough concept of academic librarianship ever to be promulgated. The movement's lack of development is exemplified by the fact that Louis Shores, who surely must be called the granddaddy of the concept, wrote essentially the same article in the March 1971 issue of *School and Society*[9]—although he changed some of the wording, defining the concept as the library-university—as he published in the January 26, 1935, issue of that magazine. (Indeed, most articles on the library-college concept sound vaguely alike.)

In highly simplified terms, the concept moves the teaching/learning responsibility from the faculty and classroom into the library for independent study by students. Practicalities aside, it is the only clear-cut philosophical statement of service with accompanying objectives of how academic libraries can support the educational trends of this century, for example, student-centered learning, multiple approaches to the curriculum, interdisciplinary studies, and independent study. It is this ability to comprehend the grand view of higher education and its goals, together with the ultimate conceptualization of the library's role in the total effort, that is so desperately needed today.

There is no question but that the basic principles of the library-college concept are in alignment with current reforms in higher education. That it is one of the few ideas of value in dealing with contemporary library service is attested to by its being singled out (along with Patricia Knapp's experiment at Montieth) for mention in the pertinent section of the National Advisory Commission on Libraries' resource book, *Libraries at Large*.[10] Thus it is doubly unfortunate that devotees of the library-college concept have had so little opportunity to put their theories into practice, so that meaningful experimentation and evaluation could be combined with their theories.

The ultimate failure of the library-college movement, however, grows out of its very strength, for its supporters, having found *a* way, in their enthusiasm and dedication seemingly have made it *the* way. This zeal is regrettable since implementation of the concept has obvious limitations relating to the size and scope of academic institutions. Moreover, the single-minded zeal of its supporters tends to alienate both librarians and teaching faculty.

More recently, in the past ten years or so, another enthusiastic academic library movement has gotten under way. It centers on programs of library instruction and seems destined to grow in strength and followers in the coming years. Library instruction will be dealt with in a later chapter, but it should be noted here that in some respects the library-instruction trend has developed in almost reverse manner to the library-college movement. The latter began with a "name" who developed the theoretical base and with whom the movement is still strongly associated. The former sprang up as a grass-roots effort at many institutions across the country; it has no theoretical base nor any movementwide goals, and although a few "names" are often associated with "library instruction" they are for the most part public service or middle-management personnel who do not have national reputations in the profession.

It would seem, then, that the library-college movement and the library-instruction trend have much to offer each other. One has the experience of operating from the top (theory) down and the other from the bottom (on-the-job application) up. Since both are uniquely concerned with aligning library services and the educational goals of their institutions, it is to be hoped that the two may join, instead of everyone's staying with his or her "thing." Indeed, the chapters that follow offer a third model for library activists—one that may prove to be built upon the strengths of both earlier models. This new model may also help initiate a new terminology that will not alienate students, faculty, administrators, and other librarians as "library college" and "library instruction" do.

In the meantime, there can be no doubt that open admissions policies present a unique challenge to academic libraries: to assume their rightful and necessary position in the educational scene, not in terms of status but in terms of service to students and, indeed, as a pacesetter in that service. Status will follow as the day does the night.

CHAPTER FIVE

The Disadvantaged Students

•

Who Are They and What Do They Want?

Having by one means or another arrived at the topic of open admissions several times, it is time for us to look more closely at the phenomenon in terms now not so much of methods, procedures, or even challenges but of the new clientele it brings to campuses. We are told that we are dealing with high school graduates who are, at the same time, educationally disadvantaged. Without intellectually accepting the failure of the American educational system, one is faced with an anomaly of major proportions. Once one accepts the fact that the twelve or more years of public education represented by a high school diploma do not necessarily imply much learning of subject matter or communications skills, one is ready to acknowledge, if not comprehend, the disadvantaged college student: a young person, who may be an apt student of life, and wise beyond his or her years in survival tactics, but one who is singularly lacking in the most elementary learning skills.

Such an understanding is essential to a discussion of open admissions students, since hard data on their intellectual potential and academic abilities are not known. IQ scores (as will be discussed in chapter 7) are known to have negligible values in evaluating such students. Perhaps the most pertinent information to emerge from the New York City situation is the recent (albeit indirect) acknowledgment that large numbers of its high school graduates do not posses eighth-grade-level reading or mathematics abilities.[1] Of those who have received high school diplomas, many do not have even junior high-level communications or mathematics skills.

Such limitations are manifested in many ways. For example, readers of this book discerned within two minutes of picking it up whether it is of interest or use to them. Our procedures in doing this are so habitual that we hardly notice them: a glance at the table of contents, the index and bibliography, the copyright date, and probably the blurb about the author. These are *not* the procedures of the disadvantaged student. Although never the subject of a controlled study, there seems to be a direct relationship between students' poor academic abilities, in particular their difficulty in reading, and the likelihood of their picking up the first book they find on the topic of interest, starting with the first word in chapter 1, and painstakingly, word by word, laboring through the book, or, frustrated by a lack of understanding or the inappropriateness of the information, they throw the book aside.

This inability of educationally disadvantaged students to assess information quickly and the difficulties under which they labor in absorbing it reinforces a pattern they have experienced all their lives: inability to beat the system, the system that overwhelms them. If we compound this with the fact that they are not sure that they even like the system, much less want to relate to it, we can understand the frustration they face daily.

But who are the open admissions students? What do they want? What do they need? A search of educational literature and the popular press provides generalities about this heterogeneous group of individuals who are called open admissions students. The writings from the paraprofessional or New Careerist movement of the sixties' war on poverty supplies additional insights.

Literally, "open admissions student" refers to every student who is admitted to a college that has an open admissions policy—both the academically prepared and the educationally disadvantaged. Popularly, and throughout this book, however, "open admissions student" refers to the educationally disadvantaged student who would not have been admitted to an academic program under traditional criteria.

First of all, and contrary to popular opinion, more lower- and middle-class white students than minority students have benefited from the policy of open admissions. Many of them receive a subsidy from governmental funds. In New York State during the 1973/74 academic year, for example, 27,600 educationally disadvantaged students received financial support from federal and state programs in pursuing academic programs. Most of these students were under 25, 65 percent were black, and very few were part-time students.[2]

A compilation of descriptions of attitudes and lifestyles, which was prepared in 1970 to aid paraprofessional instructors and employees, adds much to this picture of open admissions students.

Attitudes and Life Styles
of
Educationally Disadvantaged Students

1. Have a life style which is basically expressive. They derive little security from family or institutional relationships. Consequently, they are not socialized to seek solutions to problems through organizations.
2. Tend to be fatalistic about an individual's ability to affect his life in any major or significant way.
3. Approach the job situation with a mixture of motives. Most have self-centered reasons for becoming paraprofessionals. Altruism is not an important consideration.
4. Because of demographic background they can move freely in a community. There is no need to be concerned about validating themselves to clients.
5. Tend not to be judgmental and moralistic with respect to behavior such as drinking, illegitimacy, continuous unemployment.
6. Tend to be quite direct and oriented toward taking quick action. Tend to be impatient with delays and a good deal of verbal behavior.
7. Place more emphasis on external life circumstances than on internal characteristics of people. Consequently, they see problems more as externally caused than the result of internal deficiencies.
8. Likely to be skeptical and suspicious of bureaucratic authority. This comes from both lack of experience with organizations and from past histories of exploitation.
9. Have a basic work style which tends to be informal. Place little emphasis on formal constraints like channels of communication and confidential data. Tend more toward congeniality and friendliness than toward objectivity and detachment.
10. Have an eclectic and pragmatic approach to problem solving. This results in spontaneity and impatience with heavy emphasis on methodology.
11. Likely to be more comfortable with concrete tasks, problems, and methods. Impatient with abstractions.
12. Are impatient with planning activities. Tend also to view plans as promises.[3]

An understanding of the academic background of these students is also essential. It is a well-known fact that the range between the good and the poor students grows throughout the elementary and high school years, so that by the time they are ready to begin college the spread of competency levels has stretched to eleven years or more.[4] (One of the serious recommendations for alleviating CUNY's budgetary problems during New York City's financial crisis in 1975 was to require high school graduates to give evidence of eighth-grade English and mathematics abilities to qualify for college admission.[5]) This wide variance in academic ability among holders of high school diplomas presents two very real dilemmas at the college level.

First, how can one cope with such diversity of ability and present an educational program that is meaningful to all? On this point the literature on open admissions is clear: remedial programs, both in and out of the classroom, must be implemented so that the open admissions students can be prepared for regular academic offerings. Since one aspect of such remedial programs is at the heart of this book and since general considerations of remedial programs were given in chapter 2, little will be said on this point at this time, other than calling attention to some areas of psychological conflict.

The need for support or remedial programs has often led to channeling open admissions students into special programs; where this occurs, students often suffer from negative psychological effects.[6] Many of the students may have feelings of meaninglessness, powerlessness, and alienation from the campus mainstream, or feel that the college is establishing a ghetto on the campus.[7] Moreover, since one's achievement is strongly influenced by the aspirations and educational background of other students,[8] such channeling may deprive disadvantaged students of the peer relationships which could benefit them the most.

This brings us to the second dilemma: despite the low academic achievement of open admissions students, educators who are involved with such programs agree that one of the basic premises which must be accepted for successful educational endeavors with disadvantaged students is that the students are capable and intelligent and can "handle" a college education. They are not inferior people; rather, they are "different," because they have had to be "different" to survive.[9]

This question of respect for the ability and value of the students is important not only for those who work with them; it is crucial for the students. There is a strong relationship between the disadvantaged student's self-concept and the likelihood of his being successful in college. Indeed, the disadvantaged student's motivation stems from feelings of self-worth, as opposed to social evaluation as the source of motivation for the academically prepared student.[10] If the disadvantaged student's concept of his or her academic ability is enhanced, higher academic achievement will result, whereas a history of academic failures jeopardizes such self-confidence. This cycle of failure must be broken by a successful academic experience that offers opportunity for the individual to utilize to the fullest his capabilities and desires.[11]

The difficulty in the disadvantaged minority students' achieving success is intensified by social and cultural pressures and by not having firsthand models after which to pattern their academic and career goals. They are caught between two cultures: the ethnic and racial community on one hand

and the establishment on the other. They not only bear the burden of personal achievement under almost overwhelming odds (thus the label "disadvantaged" by the establishment) but are seen as extraordinarily advantaged by their own community. Their success or failure is seen as the success or failure of the community. Add to this the fact that, at the same time, they are pressured to conform to establishment rules and procedures and, by their ethnic community, to emphasize and cultivate its distinguishing traits as signs of new-found pride and self-esteem.[12] The disadvantaged student must become both a psychologist and a philosopher to cope with such conflicting loyalties, and on top of this the student is expected to learn!

There is also a serious lack in the disadvantaged student's life—particularly the minority student—of personally known and/or ethnic-related images upon which to pattern higher-education goals, nor will there be many such images until the first groups of open admissions students from one's neighborhood have succeeded in graduating and going on to fulfilling careers.[13] Indeed, the seeking of goals so different from those of one's family and peers can lead to loss of friendship and antagonism, for if the goals of the college-bound student are correct, does this not necessitate that his family and friends be left behind for new commitments?

Such conflicts and the lack of models in the life of educationally disadvantaged college students often lead to role ambiguity or lack of role identification. They do not know who they are or who they are becoming, and their educational experiences must, at least, provide an opportunity to discover who they are.[14] Unless this opportunity is provided early enough, disadvantaged students will probably face far too much anxiety (engendered by lack of role identity) for learning to be effective.[15] The educational goal that will best serve them is not assimilation (loss of assured identity) but integration (freedom to move, relate, and interrelate while retaining their ethnic, racial, and cultural identity).[16]

Scholastic motivation, adequate study skills, and a supportive social environment, then, are the factors which determine academic success, but these are the very conditions which have been absent from the disadvantaged student's background. The primary objective of academic programs, therefore, must be to create such conditions in order to break the failure pattern of these students.[17] Obviously, there is a particular need for improving the quality of the freshman year of college in order to keep young people from dropping out of school.[18] In turn, breaking the failure pattern provides, in and of itself, the greatest scholastic motivation.[19] Motivation, not intelligence, is the critical factor for academic success in higher education.[20]

To make such conditions possible and thus ensure the success of open admissions programs, it is generally acknowledged that three elements are required: student financial aid, personal and academic counseling, and a remedial support program. The importance of these elements cannot be overestimated; however, for obvious reasons, only the latter is dealt with directly in the following chapters.

If the students who enter open admissions colleges have particular problems, they also have special things going for them. In most cases their enrollment represents personal and family sacrifice, so that there is no such thing as an apathetic open admissions student (the student who cannot cope with a particular course or situation will often quietly drop out). These students haven't taken a college education for granted and are more than willing to "pay their dues" for the opportunity. Given the support they need to make the most of their chance of success, they not only work for that success but do so with zest, with each positive experience reinforcing the likelihood of the next success.

Along with the zest, however, is a low level of tolerance for the traditionalism and ivory tower aspects of higher education. They are less willing to play a "game" than many other students, though, in fact, many white middle-class students joined with minority groups in pressing for open admissions policies as a means of forcing innovation in their own college programs.[21] This impatience is also fed by the growing sense of consumer rights in education.[22]

A second big plus for academically disadvantaged students (see item 9 in the attitudes list) is their less-than-normal tendency toward a competitive attitude, which can be seen in their support of each other's work. This atmosphere can provide formal and informal peer-tutorial opportunities that have excellent educational benefits, as well as the supportive social environment that is required for their academic success.

Educationally disadvantaged students, then—insofar as any group can be generalized—cannot be characterized by their ethnic or cultural background or by their level of intelligence or academic mastery. However, they are easily discouraged, are often impatient, and need basic support by way of financial aid, counseling, and—particularly in communications skills—remedial training. They are willing, if they can see a way, to fight to survive in the academic world, as in their home environment.

CHAPTER SIX

Library
Instruction • Old and New
• Approaches

Given the challenge that open admissions policies offer academic libraries and a basic, if superficial, understanding of educationally disadvantaged students, the next logical step is for librarians to evaluate their services in light of these new and/or expanding needs. Surely there is an obvious and immediate need for a program of library instruction to provide the remedial assistance that open admissions students require in order to survive in an academic setting—if not, also, to better survive in their total life experiences. What programs and patterns of library instruction can be utilized or modified for this purpose? With the increased importance of library instruction on many campuses in recent years, what instructional approaches have proved to be most effective?

Actually, there is a long history of library instruction to call upon. Yet, unfortunately, library instruction is one of the profession's most persisting problems. There is much literature on the subject, but it does not impress one with its quality.[1] This is perhaps best exemplified by the fact that the most frequently employed means of academic library instruction is still the orientation tour, which is traditionally held during the freshman year. A survey of academic libraries in New York State, for example, showed that 80 percent of the responding libraries give such tours.[2] Nevertheless, one of the few points of agreement in the literature is the almost obvious fact that a student's first weeks at college are not the best time for library instruction. Students are too preoccupied with adjusting to their instructors and classes, as well as college life in general, to do more than stoically submit to the demanded library tour.[3]

Besides the tour, other elements of instruction in college libraries are lectures on the card catalog and indexes, as well as, perhaps, a bibliographic lecture on a particular subject for an advanced undergraduate or graduate course. In elementary and secondary schools this repertoire includes lessons on how to use an encyclopedia, a dictionary, and maps. Particularly on the elementary level, introduction to certain aspects of literature as fairy tales is sometimes considered to be on the fringe of library instruction.

It is quite clear that traditional library instruction has tended to focus on particular tools or resources in the library. Little consideration has been given to search strategies or techniques of information evaluation, or even to the students themselves. Traditional library instruction is usually apart from the subject-related projects of the students, and there has been little concern for evaluating the effectiveness of such activities.

The tragedy of this situation was demonstrated in an alumni-day discussion group at Columbia, in the spring of 1972, with representatives from all levels of school and academic libraries, plus some public librarians. The elementary librarians explained how they taught basic library skills to their students, but the junior high librarians said that was impossible, for when students reached junior high they had no library knowledge and had to be taught basic skills. Needless to say, the story was repeated by the academic librarians, and the public librarians added that few of their users knew even the most elementary skills. Obviously, from the user's viewpoint, better library instruction is a very real need.

Some library instructional attempts are actually disastrous and do harm rather than good, as, for example, one of the first attempts at library instruction for educationally disadvantaged students at Brooklyn College during the summer of 1970. The basic-skills experience which was planned for this first group of open admissions students, before their entrance into regular undergraduate classes, was planned to emphasize writing skills; library skills were a minor consideration.[4] The instruction in the latter consisted of a library assignment that was designed without the assistance of a librarian, included such questions as "What are the differences between the Library of Congress and the Dewey Classification systems?" and was due before the scheduled library tours. Had the department head and the instructors tried to construct an initial exposure to the college library calculated to create abhorrence of the library, they could not have done better.

One of the best surveys of methods of library instruction is Frances Henne's "Instruction in the Use of Libraries and Library Use by Students."[5] John Lubans's *Educating the Library User*,[6] which focuses on the rationale and techniques in establishing a vital, ongoing relationship between libraries and clientele, is one of the newest and best overviews of library instruction, for the problems in library instruction go far beyond the lessons and include such topics as faculty cooperation and human and social interactions.

In reading the literature one finds five basic methods of library instruction: course-related library instruction, a separate course, point-of-use audiovisual aids, handout guides, and television teaching. But for most academic library situations, only the first two methods are seen as of practical value in educating students for effective library use, and the first method requires great effort to get students to enroll, plus a librarian with exceptional enthusiasm and talent for teaching.[7]

There is no doubt, however, that in the ranks of academic librarians there is enough talent and ability for almost any type of instructional program. A survey of CUNY librarians in the spring of 1971, for example, revealed that

> Of the total of 348 librarians in CUNY four percent have doctorates, 55 percent have graduate degrees in fields other than library science, 26 percent are studying for an additional graduate degree, and another 10 percent are taking graduate courses in specialized fields. The subjects in which librarians hold graduate degrees range widely . . . 42 percent of the librarians have teaching experience, and one third of those have been teaching for more than five years, and over 40 percent have published research or edited publications in library science and other fields.[8]

Perhaps even more important than academic credentials for such teaching are personal qualities, such as being student oriented, flexible, and having a sense of humor and "a warm outgoing nature that can win over the indifferent and those who virtually dare you to say something worth listening to."[9]

No name is more closely associated with library instruction or more revered than that of Patricia B. Knapp. Her experiment in library instruction at Wayne State University is the most comprehensive study of the role of library-based instruction in a university's educational program. Usually referred to as the Montieth experiment, it is a carefully formulated curriculum design that was adopted by a college administration, in connection with library personnel, to provide a learning experience centered on independent study.[10]

Unique to this program is the concept that the "general pattern of the organization of scholarship" should be systematically taught on the undergraduate level. The library as a system of bibliographic organization is the theoretical framework for the library instruction, and the program was a sequence of assignments through a four-year undergraduate curriculum and across three subject areas. The library assignments resulted from heavy collaboration between librarians and the teaching faculty. However, the program never produced its anticipated results because the faculty that was recruited for the college, although informed of the projected independent study emphasis of the college, eventually followed more traditional patterns in their teaching.

Yet the program produced some results that are well worth noting. A definite relationship was proved between exposure to library instruction and long-range performance; that is, a statistically significant association was found between exposure and meeting degree requirements on time, and an association was indicated between exposure and maintaining a good honor point average.[11]

Again, this study is the best analysis of a major attempt at library involvement in the educational process of an institution of higher learning, and Patricia Knapp's numerous other writings on the topic also are among the best in the literature. Her efforts may well prove to be the turning point in the history of library-based instruction.

Only two other comprehensive and forward-looking attempts to relate the role of the library and library instruction to the educational goals of academic institutions—to such an extent as to involve cooperative planning by administrators, faculty, and librarians—have been noted in the literature. At Swarthmore College in Pennsylvania, the objective for library instruction was that experience and proficiency in the use of library materials be made an integral part of courses.[12] The heart of the Swarthmore "teaching library" eventually became the concept of the divisional librarian, who was to "provide faculty with counseling in the bibliographical aspects of teaching and . . . give assistance to students preparing research courses and independent study projects."[13] Appointment of the first divisional librarian was made possible by a $40,000 grant, awarded jointly by the Council on Library Resources and the National Endowment for the Humanities in 1971. More than in most institutions, the profession has been able to share in Swarthmore's planning and decision-making processes, and ongoing reports on the implementation and evaluation of its teaching library are greatly desired.

In the fall of 1975, almost ten years after the conceptualization of Swarthmore's increased library commitment, an article in the new *Journal of Academic Librarianship* outlined a library program at Sangamon State in Springfield, Illinois, which boasted a full complement of instructional services librarians (ISLs).[14] One of the stated mandates of the new upper-division and graduate institution, which was founded in 1970, was innovation in higher education. Accordingly, the president sought a librarian who would develop a library program which would begin where Patricia Knapp's work left off. The library, which developed under Howard Dillon, was structured to free the professional staff (save the head of the library) from administrative duties so that they could work full time with faculty and students. The resultant ISLs represent the first corps of teaching librarians, and their success was attested to by the North Central Association's library committee report of 1974, by an independent library study commissioned by the university in 1975, and by the university's upgrading of the position of university librarian to dean of library services in 1975. Despite little publicity about the Sangamon State University program, other libraries have begun to modify their administrative structures to facilitate instructional commitments along the lines of the SSU library.

The library instructional program is multifaceted. An ISL is a member of every program (department) committee on the campus and, as such, is party to all curriculum planning. An ISL is on duty at all times at the Get Help Here Desk on the main floor of the library. Each semester numerous general workshops, as well as workshops in conjunction with the informational needs of particular courses, are held. In the fall of 1976, workshops for university secretaries and all campus graduate assistants were offered for the first time, and the ISLs have offered a credit-bearing course as well as credit-bearing tutorials for individual students. Beyond this, and perhaps most significantly, a number of the programs have adopted "library literacy" as part of their graduation requirements.

In all three of these innovative programs a great deal of faculty cooperation was essential, and yet the realities of the commitment to and participation in even traditional and limited programs of library instruction (much less the more ambitious ones just cited) within the library profession itself are confused at best.[15] The published results of the world library press concerning the problems of library and bibliographical instruction have been so varied that it is difficult to find any general accord, except that library instruction fares best when there is collaboration between the administrations of the college and the library.[16] Surveys of actual practices show great variation within any area and provide, at most, vague suggestions of general trends. For the most part, the literature deals with how libraries "do their thing" in library instruction. Moreover, just as all librarians do not support the library-college concept, not all librarians are convinced of the validity of libraries' participating in the teaching function of their institutions. Yet, until some consensus of commitment to the concept of library-based instruction can be reached by academic librarians on a particular campus, little or no progress in achieving faculty cooperation can realistically be expected.

If libraries have yet to meet the instructional challenge of academically prepared students, there is, even more frequently, an acknowledgment of their failure to meet the special needs of educationally disadvantaged students, who must be helped to understand, use, and quickly profit from their contact with librarians and the library.[17]

Allen Ballard, as dean of academic affairs for CUNY, saw this failure—what was basically considered a denial of knowledge and access to knowledge—as an underlying cause of unrest among black students in the late sixties. Since the only place one can begin in any objective and systematic fashion to obtain knowledge is in a library, Ballard urged that there be some connection between the turmoil on the campuses and what the libraries were doing and were planning to do.[18]

Despite this acknowledged need for a revitalized role for libraries in current educational programs and the picture of the library as the heart of the university, current changes and trends in academia are granted only a passing reference in library literature, and library participation in the remedial programs that are offered on many campuses, if it occurs, is not reported.[19] Such failure on the part of libraries became especially crucial with the advent of open admissions policies, because disadvantaged students in particular do not know what to expect or what to ask in the way of support from libraries or librarians, which makes it impossible for them to understand, much less express, their informational needs.[20]

There is, however, some material on the work of academic libraries with educationally disadvantaged students. John Lubans, director of public services for the University of Colorado libraries, conducted research into the library use patterns of disadvantaged freshmen, compared with regular freshmen, in 1968. He concluded: "It would appear from the A.O. [Academic Opportunity] student's pattern of use of the Rensselaer Library as well as his willingness and ability to grade library services and facilities that the library does play more of a role in the A.O. student's life than in that of the non-A.O. student."[21] Library instruction for academically disadvantaged Chicano students at the Los Angeles campus of the University of California, through a self-study approach,[22] and its expansion to academically prepared college freshmen have been detailed in library literature by Miriam Dudley,[23] and three self-study manuals have been developed, published, and marketed as a result of this work.[24]

Another example of library-based instruction describes the results of a basic English course at Upsala College in East Orange, New Jersey, when it was restructured to include extensive library involvement. The overall class performance went up, but of particular interest is the fact that the overall improvement and the caliber of work of the eight high-risk students in the class exceeded the class average.[25]

Although library work with disadvantaged students in the City University of New York was officially under way considerably before the beginning of open admissions, there have been only two published accounts of such work. At a conference sponsored by the Library Association of the City University of New York on April 10, 1969, on the topic "A New College Student: The Challenge to City University Libraries," Mordine Mallory, the SEEK librarian at Queens College, reported on her work,[26] and in a *Library Journal* article in September of the following year, Sylvia Wright reported on her work as a SEEK librarian for City College.[27]

The approaches in these situations varied considerably, but the general success of the programs, as evidenced by the enthusiasm they engendered (no testing was done of the program's effect on the academic success of the students involved), seem to imply a receptiveness on the part of disadvantaged students and faculty that was not generally evidenced in even such well-planned library-related learning experiences as the Montieth experiment.

By and large, the "major impression one receives from reviewing the literature on library service for undergraduate education is that a great deal more is said about what ought to be done than about what is actually being done. Further, there are many more plans, described in glowing terms, than there are reports on their implementation. Real evaluation of the effectiveness of new programs is almost nonexistent."[28]

Perhaps the problem is much more elementary. Perhaps the only way a clean transition can be made from old to new approaches to library instruction is to change the term "library instruction." No one—but no one—is interested in "library instruction." What people are interested in is the information to solve or meet their immediate problems. We hope that as interest and work in library instruction expands, a euphemism may be found. Besides being vague (don't we give library instruction in library schools?), "library instruction" is certainly not a term that elicits interest from many librarians, much less administrators, faculty, or students. "Individualization of communication controls" or even "information-handling skills" has something that "library instruction" doesn't, and maybe that's the best place to begin.

Certainly there is growing concern across the country for better library instruction. The American Library Association established the Instruction in the Use of Libraries Committee in 1967. At the ALA Convention in Chicago in June 1972, this committee sponsored an exhibit of library instruction materials from all types of libraries across the country. The exhibit filled a two-room suite, was open for one evening and the following morning, and an attendance of about 500 was anticipated for these two periods. To the committee's astonishment, within fifteen minutes of the opening of the exhibit more than 1,500 people had crowded into the area, making it almost impossible to view the materials but suggesting that many librarians are facing up to this need as never before.

It would have greatly simplified the problems facing librarians who are newly involved with programs of open admissions if the library profession had heretofore come to grips with the question of library instruction. What now seems likely is that these librarians will be the trail blazers in this important area and that the techniques and programs they develop will be the prototypes for library instruction to all students. Certainly there is a precedence for this, both in the educational literature in general and in the development of the self-study program in library instruction at the University of California at Los Angeles.

CHAPTER SEVEN

Formula for Success

●

●

With the launching of open admissions in the City University of New York in 1970, the question was what role, if any, could the library play in the academic success of the educationally disadvantaged student? At a time when higher education was seeking new answers to new problems, did the library—traditionally conceived as the heart, the center, of the learning enterprise—have anything to offer other than its traditional functions? If, in fact, the key to the success of these students is the mastering of communication skills and an enhanced self-image, of what direct help could the library and its staff be? Speaking and writing with confidence is always difficult. How could the library help students accomplish this?

If the weight of tradition spoke against the ability of academic librarians to fulfill such a role, a partnership role with their fellow educators, there were enough indications in library literature that librarians could contribute to the academic success of disadvantaged students to offer a real challenge to academic libraries at this turning point in educational history. The fact that the open admissions policy in New York City had created an atmosphere much more conducive to experimentation and to new inputs by the support units of the academic scene made it an opportunity too valuable to pass up.

Of course, there was no clear-cut way in which to proceed. What seemed essential was somehow to validate, for better or for worse, whether under certain conditions the library could play an active role in furthering the academic success of disadvantaged college freshmen. It would be better to try something and find that it was not successful, so that it could be discarded as an approach, and go on to something else, rather than again to come up with some wish-washy, indecisive results, so that neither librarian nor educator could know the value of the services being offered. If, on the other hand, an approach was tried and could be validated as having an impact for the better in the academic pursuits of the disadvantaged students, there would be something concrete on which to build.

Thus, with open admissions formally under way in CUNY, it seemed that a controlled experiment to determine whether library-based instruction could affect educational improvement was called for,[1] and in conjunction with a basic English course, since all entering freshmen were given tests in mathematics and English and were placed accordingly, in the appropriate level of instruction. For example, at City College during the first year of open admissions, "of the 2,351 who completed matriculation, slightly less than one-third were placed in English 1 [to provide fundamentals of writing]. About a tenth were urged to take English 40 [to cover problems in college writing assignments]. The remaining students appeared from the placement test to need no special writing instruction."[2]

After it was decided to work in connection with the basic writing-skills course, the question arose as to what the library could or should expect to contribute to the students' learning experience. Since satisfactory grades and "retention" were what mattered to students, faculty, and administrators, the experiment had to address these concerns. Ultimately, the experiment would succeed or fail on the basis of whether the library-based instruction had a measurable effect on the grades received and/or student retention in the basic composition course. It was this possibility that prompted the Department of Educational Services (DES) to host the experimental study.

The library input, therefore, was planned to have three primary objectives for the students: (1) to perceive informational sources, that is, libraries, as a means to success, (2) to gain ability in the use of library resources, and (3) to derive pleasure from the use of library resources. To accomplish these objectives, it was determined that the library instruction would be based on the immediate needs of the students in relation to the remedial writing course and that the instruction would be structured to assist directly in students' success in the course.

Given these three objectives, three corollaries seemed evident: (1) students had to experience success in their academic pursuits and be able to see it as a result of their library-based instruction, (2) they had to be in the library often enough to feel at home in it, and (3) they had to develop a sense of adventure about their learning process which would carry over into their use of library resources. Furthermore, once the decision was made that the instruction had to be related directly to the writing course and structured to assist in the students' success in the course, close interaction beween the librarian and the English professor was an absolute necessity, both before and during the time the course would be offered.

The most perplexing problem in designing the experiment was how to evaluate student performance. First, of course, there was the question of the students' abilities prior to their participation in the experiment. IQ, though originally scheduled for consideration, had to be eliminated, because there is general acceptance that the usual intelligence tests do not adequately measure minority students' abilities so much as the ability to read and exposure to middle-class living.[3] Even the Graduate Record Exam, which tests students after their undergraduate work, and which should serve as a leveling device, cautions: "It cannot be emphasized too often that uncritical use of test scores as forecasts of individual student's future performance is always inappropriate, but especially so far as students handicapped in their earlier educational preparation."[4]

While there was consensus among open admissions educators that new and more accurate testing indicators needed to be developed,[5] CUNY had its own criteria for determining whether students entered one of the four-year colleges or one of the two-year programs. Based on high school average or rank in class, whichever was higher, students with 85 percent or better grade averages or those in the top 30 percent of their graduating classes were admitted to the four-year colleges.

Besides the admissions criteria, placement tests were given. During the first fall of open admissions, upon entrance to any unit of CUNY, all students were given special verbal and mathematical tests, and these tests, interestingly enough, proved beyond question that traditional admission standards were not infallible, because about half of the 35,000 freshmen who took the tests needed some kind of basic remediation—not merely the 9,000 who had entered under open admissions.[6] However, since high school grade averages were one of the main CUNY criteria for college placement, it was decided to use them as one of the measuring devices of student ability prior to the library experiment. In addition, since various high schools are known as "good" or "bad," the high schools of the students were considered.

The English placement exam, which was automatically administered to all entering students, was an effective method of roughly equating student ability since it grouped students of similar writing competencies. At this point it was decided to conduct the experiment at Brooklyn College, because I had previously worked there and because the grading system for its exam separated students into six categories, ranging from 1A, indicating high proficiency in English composition and exemption from English 1.2, to 3B, indicating a severe bilingual problem and assignment to a Q section of English 0.1. Students who receive 2A are characterized as having special problems that are not of a bilingual nature and are assigned to Q sections of English 1.2. This latter group would be the concern of the experiment, and Justin L. Dunn, assistant dean of students and director of admissions for Brooklyn College, summarized the implication of the freshmen English placement on the population that was being studied: "The students' academic abilities as manifested in writing skills, insofar as can be determined by an examination, are quite similar."[7]

How to evaluate student progress over the semester of the experiment was not an easy decision. Standard library tests had acknowledged shortcomings,[8] which would only be intensified by the fact that objective tests are widely acknowledged to be invalid measurements for disadvantaged students. Again, CUNY practice gave some guidance. All the CUNY English placement tests were designed to include writing samples as they are held to be more valid measurements of ability, because they show a student's real command of the language.[9] The Brooklyn College English placement exam for the past several years had been a forty-minute composition on a topic chosen from four suggested topics. The directions for the essay note that "this is *not* an admissions test: we merely want a sample of your writing. We are mainly interested in your ability to find reasonably mature, *honest* things to say in clear, grammatical sentences and in correctly spelled, reasonably adult, *vivid* language." Adoption of this type of measurement to determine the value of the library input was deemed the most appropriate, as the instruction was tied to the basic-skills writing course, and support for this approach was found in the Montieth experiment (a main objective of which was a series of instruments for evaluating student attainment of library understanding and competence), which focused on bibliographic reviews and term papers for grading purposes.[10]

Thus it was decided that academic success was to be evidenced by residual gains in the scores between homework papers defending a self-chosen proposition (the satisfactory performance of which is the goal of the course), which were to be assigned during the first and next-to-final weeks of the semester, and that no library tests, per se, should be given. However, this procedure would necessitate a control group which would not receive the library-based instruction, so as to determine the relationship of the library to the students' success.

Meanwhile, matching the "before" and "after" mean scores for each student measured the gain in competence as accurately as possible within the bounds of an experiment. However, it was acknowledged that, as with all testing procedures, there is a likelihood of inaccuracies in actual measurements due to particular circumstances in students' lives, for example, illness, family problems at the time of the assignments, and the like. Therefore records were to be kept of the students' grades in the English course and their overall grades for the semester of the experiment and the following semester. The most important consideration was the desire to ensure, insofar as possible, that should the experiment prove successful—that is, if the library-based instruction proved to affect academic success positively—the results would be acceptable to the faculty. There is, obviously, no measure of educational achievement more likely to be accepted as valid by faculty members than faculty judgment.[11]

Since the third objective was for the students to "derive pleasure from the use of library resources," which in practical terms would mean the self-assurance so often cited as necessary to the academic success of educationally disadvantaged students, a project was included in the experimental design to see what (if any) change would occur in student use and attitude vis-à-vis the library and its resources. To determine such change, an IBM card-questionnaire, which was developed and used to determine library use patterns at the University of Colorado,[12] was changed in very minute ways to meet the needs of the situation. The questionnaires were to be administered by the professors, so that no psychological pressure would be exerted by my presence. Group interviews were arranged to elicit pertinent responses for program evaluation and future program planning.

After the objectives of the library-based instruction, the evaluative procedures for determining academic success, and the role of the library-based instruction in that success were determined, the next question was what should be taught as a supplement to the remedial writing course. This proved to be the most difficult problem, next to determining the evaluative procedures for the experiment. Available library literature was not detailed enough for use, or was geared to elementary or high school situations, or, perhaps most inappropriately (according to the initial concept of basing the instruction on the immediate needs of the students in relation to the remedial writing course), seemed to approach library-related skills as ends in themselves. There seemed to be nothing to do but to develop materials from scratch.

Analysis of open admissions literature provided general guidelines for the development of instruction materials for the experiment, and seemed to point to the unique ability of the library to meet the particular needs of disadvantaged students. For example, the students did not like to be stigmatized as belonging to a disadvantaged group,[13] so that, whenever possible, remedial and compensatory upgrading should be achieved at an individualized pace and with minimum institutionalization.[14] Nor should the students be pushed toward a single, predetermined goal.[15] Flexibility and individualization were essential.[16]

Two other general imperatives were clearly outlined in open admissions curriculum studies: the work should build on the basis of the students' needs and characteristics, as well as those of their society, and the instruction should furnish a clear demonstration of the kind of problems the subject deals with, how it is organized, and how it relates to their other studies.[17] Based on the literature on library instruction, the decision had already been made that library input should be as closely related to the immediate concerns of the English 1.2 curriculum as possible, and these directives from the literature on remedial instruction reinforced this concept. Thus, although the couse content and the professors' teaching styles were studied before the beginning of the experiment, library input, for the most part, had to be developed as the course went on.

Several principles were carefully followed in the class sessions and in the weekly handouts:

1. *The information to be covered should be approached from the viewpoint of student need,* and not that of a well-rounded library and research skills program. This meant that much attention was paid to areas not traditionally considered the perogative of libraries, for example, how to determine main ideas in books and articles.

2. *No library tools should be taught per se,* but only as means to success in the course. Therefore, card catalog analytics, including subject tracings, were discussed at length for the help they could provide in evaluating available materials' value in relation to research needs, but atlases were never mentioned.

3. *Students should be taught to evaluate the usefulness for their individual writing assignments of one type of information over another.* Thus they contrasted information in *Collier's Encyclopedia* with the *World Book,* the information in the pamphlet file with that in books (and only incidentally—see point 2—learned how to use these tools).

4. *The information covered should have immediate application* through hands-on use and, when possible, adaptability into that week's writing assignment.

5. *Students should be exposed to the wide variety of materials available in a library;* for example, every student looked at a different specialized dictionary and shared what he found with his class.

6. *Students should be shown methods for handling information;* for example, a system for taking notes on 3 by 5-inch cards was demonstrated.

Although the classroom discussions are not available for analysis of these principles "in action," the sample worksheets in appendix 3 are somewhat illustrative.

In simplest terms, the experiment provided that three similar groups of educationally disadvantaged students would receive varying degrees of library-based instruction as supplementary support to their remedial writing courses. The basic experiment was planned as a one hour per week session of library and information retrieval assistance which would emphasize information collection skills and facility in the evaluation of resources in relation to the remedial writing course. This weekly instruction was to be housed in the library, but had to be kept in synchronization with the English instruction by regular meetings with the professor. This instruction was to be given in addition to the time normally allotted the English course. One of the professor's sections would be a control group and would not receive any library instruction whatsoever.

The experiment was to include a more traditional type of library instruction, that is, an orientation tour of the library and lectures on the use of the card catalog and indexes. This seemed necessary since it is the type of instruction most often provided and would answer the question whether an intermediate amount of library input (somewhere between the weekly instruction and no instruction at all) might not prove equally satisfactory. To accomplish this, a second professor had to be added to the experiment. One of this professor's sections received the prescribed three hours of traditional library instruction, which was administered by me and replaced three hours of regularly scheduled class time. (To keep the English instruction input constant for every section in the experiment, each section that did not receive the traditional library instruction was asked to record at least three hours of class time, which were characterized not by instruction but by informal student interaction.) Another section of the second professor was held as a control group. To add to the number of students and to make sure that any difference in results could not be accounted for by the difference in professors, the experiment was extended to a second semester and the type of library instruction was switched between the professors.

The weekly instruction was normally to consist of a brief period of explanation and a lab session. The topics were chosen and a tentative order for their presentation was established by the individual professor and myself prior to the beginning of each semester. Although they would be modified from time to time, a composite list of the topics to be covered (exclusive of the variations due to the professors' teaching styles and the particular strengths and weaknesses of the classes) is as follows:

1. *Importance of information* to academic and future success; a tour of the Brooklyn College library
2. *Main ideas;* abstracts from books and articles, book and play synopses
3. *Picking topics* for papers and speeches

4. *Parts of books;* use in obtaining information prior to reading text
5. *Dictionaries;* how and why to use them when writing papers; variety of
6. *Encyclopedias;* how and why to use them in writing papers; comparison of
7 & 8. *Reader's Guide;* how and why to use it in writing papers; variations of
9. *New York Times Index and the pamphlet file;* how and why to use them in writing papers; comparison of variety and type of information available
10 & 11. *Card catalog;* how and why to use it in writing papers; how to evaluate materials before locating them; how to locate additional materials on a subject
12 & 13. *Collection and organization of material for research papers;* step-by-step procedure for preparing research papers, including explanation and demonstration of note-taking techniques
14. *Review of key library resources;* library-resources treasure hunt and party.

The three traditional hours of library instruction (which were given to two other groups) were to be chiefly concerned with:

1. The importance of information to academic and future success; a tour of the Brooklyn College library
2. How to locate books and evaluate their usefulness before reading them; how to take notes on book information
3. How to locate and evaluate nonbook information, with emphasis on *Reader's Guide* and special consideration of the pamphlet file and *New York Times Index;* how to take notes on periodical information.

In the final analysis, each segment of both types of library input were designed around the questions why and how. Each input was to begin with the fundamental question of why factual information is important to students' individual success in college and in their total lives. Each topic, each tool, was to be explained in relation to the total research-writing process and its particular importance pointed out so that the students knew why each item was covered. Everything was to be done to provide student motivation in terms of what-will-I-get-out-of-this, including, where appropriate, exploration of why the students should perform to the best of their abilities.

Close attention was also to be given to the very practical methods and techniques of research-writing procedures. Easy and "safe" ways of choosing topics for English papers were to be explored; how to glean maximum information from the jackets, the foreword material, chapter headings, and indexes of books was demonstrated; and how to take notes, easily and efficiently, for research papers was shown. The aim was to provide students, as painlessly as possible, all the appropriate shortcuts and techniques and the "knack" for research writing that a professional librarian could accumulate in a lifetime. The focus of attention was to be always on the subject or content of the immediate paper, with the how's being merely the means to a better paper, a better grade.

CHAPTER EIGHT

Brooklyn College • A Test Case

The Experiment

The experiment was conducted at Brooklyn College during the spring and fall 1972 semesters. A description of the students and faculty will lay the foundation for the implementation of the experiment.

A rough profile of a composite class is nine females, of whom six completed the course work, and seven males, of whom five completed the course work. For practical purposes, the individual classes did not deviate to such an extent as to make the outcome of the experiment unduly slanted by the number or sex of the participants.

Observation of the groups did not elicit concern for age variances among the participants (the students, by and large, had completed high school requirements within the preceding year or two); so age was excluded as a variable in this experiment, as had been anticipated in the proposal. The 130 students in the experiment represented sixty different high school backgrounds, including a number of students who held high school equivalencies from foreign schools or other sources. Thirty-four high school backgrounds had only one representative and two high schools had the maximum representation of seven. This wide variance in high school backgrounds made this variable worthless for evaluative purposes.

In overall academic ability of the sections, the high school averages varied from 11.0 to 88.5. However, close examination of the averages showed that a truer picture emerged by eliminating the three extreme scores on both ends, giving a range of 59.4 to 80.7, for a variance of 21.3 points and a mean high school average of 71.79. The mean high school averages for the groups varied from a low of 68.78 to a high of 73.9, or for a variance from the mean of 3.01 and 2.11 respectively—too small to be significant in the outcome. Furthermore, the experience of the Brooklyn College registrar, Charles D. Wantman, reinforced the position that the makeup of the sections in the experiment was established on a random basis so that no class would vary to any significant degree from any other in academic ability. Mr. Wantman stated:

> Students who are enrolled in Q sections of courses are not assigned to individual sections according to any specific criteria. Students are aware of the available sections, and select their own on whatever basis is appropriate to them. Normally students have a particular set of courses meeting at a particular set of times which have an impact on their selection of Q sections. It would seem to me that you could assume a random distribution of students in the various "Q" sections when looked at from the point of view of IQ scores or other kind of measurements.[1]

The greatest variance among the students, observed in the classes which received library-based instruction, was in temperament. Students ranged from seemingly eager to learn to apathetic. Following an observable pattern of educationally disadvantaged college students, some of the latter attended only at the beginning of the semester and soon dropped out of the course, and a few were irregular in attendance throughout the semester, but many never missed a session. English-class attendance paralleled the attendance in the weekly library sessions. Some students initially evidenced hostility and/or aloofness.

In the classes that received weekly library instruction, the students' basic personality traits remained consistent within the English and library-based class sessions, and in each class there were a few outstanding personalities. The key student in both cases was a woman, but there the similarity stopped. In Professor A's class the pivotal figure was an older Puerto Rican woman who had a high school equivalency degree. She was a mother figure for the class; in time, she was treated almost protectively by her classmates. For example, they were almost as much concerned that she should pass the course as they were for themselves. When it was time to plan for the final class session, this woman, entirely on her own, collected money from the other students, purchased special Spanish coffee and pastries for the occasion, and provided paper plates and napkins.

In Professor B's class the counterpart was a much younger and very attractive black girl who had graduated from Prospect Heights High School with a 74.2 average. When it came time to plan for the end-of-semester party, one of the students suggested that she should be in charge of the arrangements, which consisted of agreeing that everyone would bring their own sandwiches. It was a more independent class, and the girl's role was not so much that of group leader as acknowledged intellectual of the class.

In both classes the second-ranking leaders were men. In Professor A's class the man was a young Puerto Rican, self-assured, articulate, restless. In professor B's class the man was a young Italian, fairly quiet, with a gentle and warm disposition.

In both classes there was friendliness and openness among the students and willingness to help each other—an atmosphere which was encouraged by having the students help each other on the initial drafts of their papers. The library-based instruction capitalized on this situation by creating on-the-spot student tutoring arrangements whenever appropriate, and these proved most beneficial. The total class personality, however, varied greatly with the professor, and the classes' responses to me and their concept of the relationship between the English and the library instruction also varied greatly with the professor.

Both English professors were library oriented before their inclusion in the experiment; they were, in fact, suggested by the Department of Educational Services Librarian on the basis of their demonstrated use of the library and library resources in their previous semesters' class assignments. Their enthusiasm for the potential role of library-based instruction in the English 1.2 curriculum was proved by their volunteering to participate in the experiment, even though there would be no remuneration for the extra work it would cause them over a three-semester period.

Beyond this, the professors were different in almost every respect, and one of the most interesting aspects of the experiment was the difference between the two professors' relationships with their classes and the resultant intergroup relations of the classes.

Professor A was a sink-or-swim man; after the first few weeks, a paper was due every week. He had little patience with students who were late, absent, or failed to complete their assignments. The students who could keep up with him, and stuck with the course to the end, accomplished more than students in other sections of the course, but many students simply did not make it. His outspoken, demanding manner soon made the students in the weekly experimental class pull together as a group and draw close to me. A number of times (they came directly from English instruction) the students arrived at the library highly agitated over the class session, and these occasions presented excellent opportunities to start the lessons by pointing out what the professor had been trying to get them to accomplish and why, and how the library-related skills could help them more easily accomplish what the professor was demanding.

Their cohesiveness made assisting the students very easy, as it was quickly evident where they needed help. The constant pressure from their professor drove them to learn more in the library and gave them more desire to learn —to please me (the librarian and their "supporter") and/or in fear of the professor. They tended to view the library-based instruction as separate from their English lessons, although every effort was made to coordinate the two. A problem that arose from this professor's approach to teaching was that, by the end of both semesters, so many students had officially or unofficially dropped out of the professor's section (except his weekly experimental group) that it was extremely difficult to get the final papers and the second of the two attitude cards.

In Professor B's class the situation was almost completely reversed. Professor B nurtured her classes. She was concerned for the feelings as well as the academic accomplishments of the students and did not require nearly as much turned-in work as the other professor. The apparent result was that there were fewer dropouts, but her classes as a whole and individuals in her classes did not reach the high level of accomplishment of some from Professor A's classes. Her sections as a whole, however, made more progress than Professor A's.

Because there was no teacher-student personality conflict, Professor B's weekly experimental class did not draw particularly close together, though the students, after a time, tended to lunch together (following the library instruction period) and evidenced a desire to keep in contact with classmates in the following semester. Obviously, this class did not provide the same emotional satisfaction for me, because the students did not need to relate as closely to me as those from Professor A's class. There was, however, obvious and early appreciation for the instruction, and the students viewed the library aspects of the program as an integral part of the total course. They saw it not as an English course and a library-instruction course but as *a* course, and seemed well aware of the close interplay between the professor and me. This English professor remained the "heart" of the class throughout the semester.

It was impossible to say, as the experiment was conducted, which English professor's approach best facilitated the library-instruction inputs; however, the statistical results eventually pointed out some effects of their differing approaches in combination with the library instruction. The most important input during a semester was, of course, the instruction given by the English professors, and every effort was made to hold this content standard. For example, the four control groups received the same English instruction as the other sections, including the same verbal encouragement for using outside sources, etc., in writing their papers. They did not receive, however, library-based instruction or a tour of the Brooklyn College library.

As for the three hours of traditional library input, all but the tour was conducted in the classroom, with the professor in attendance to ensure the maximum value for this much more limited input. These sessions were scheduled entirely at the discretion of the professors and were tied as closely as possible to the research demands of each class at the points of input.

To reinforce the concept that the weekly library-based instruction was an integral part of the English course, I was introduced to the class by the English professor and addressed the class during its first meeting. The additional hour of work was explained as one of several ways in which the Department of Educational Services was trying to improve the chances of students' academic success. Students were requested not to share the benefits of the additional instruction with other English 1.2 students, as further implementation of the program would depend on their anticipated gains in performance over and above what other students accomplished. This "sales talk" was agreed upon by the professors, the Department of Educational Services librarian, and myself, to counteract a likely reaction of why-do-we-have-to-do-more-work-for-the-same-amount-of-credit? This potential problem was particularly acute in Professor A's group, as a mistake in the registering procedure had not informed the students of the additional class hour required for the course. Full registration in the expanded course the following semester confirmed the belief that an additional hour made little or no difference to students if it fit into their schedule.

The library time was divided between classroom instruction and individual library work. No library homework was assigned, but often the in-library work was directly related to the current writing assignments, so that students could, if they desired, expand their in-library work to cover their English 1.2 assignments. Every effort was made to help the students make up library sessions they missed. Normally, they would see me after the following session for the missed assignment, and the Department of Educational Services librarian was available during the week to assist them.

The professors chose not to attend any but the final hour of the weekly library instruction; however, for approximately the first two-thirds of the semester I was a guest in the English section involved in the weekly library-instruction input. This served two purposes: it enabled me to get to know the students and their needs more quickly and it served to keep the library input closely related to the material covered in the English course that week (without placing a burden on the professor for weekly progress reports).

Although the subject matter in the library instruction and samples of the materials are given elsewhere in this work, a word should be added about the instruction. The emphasis was always on the practical, including such common-sense directives as where in the library professional librarians could be found, and how to ask questions (and everyone, it was pointed out, including professional librarians, had "off days"). The Department of Educational Services librarian, who was introduced as "their" librarian, sat in on a number of classes and helped with makeup library work.

Almost every week students received a set of worksheets which was designed to reinforce the principles listed in the previous chapter, as well as to (1) highlight key facts for individual review, as needed by the students, (2) provide examples as a basis for class discussion or for completing lab assignments, and (3) provide fill-in assignment sheets for the lab portion of the class. The latter were used to minimize writing by the students so that their chief energy could be devoted to acquiring the information-handling skills, and often the information they would look up could be used for a paper they were writing. Often a class discussion outline was included in the set, not only to help students see individual facts in relation to the overall topic but to illustrate the value of organizing main ideas into logical order before beginning to write a paper. Included in the sample materials in appendix 3 are a one-page summary of course material which was used as part of a review just prior to the students' collecting and organizing material for their final research paper and a periodical worksheet set which was part of the traditional library input on locating and evaluating nonbook information. These materials were also useful in helping students catch up on material that had been covered while they were absent.

Students had the most difficulty in assignments that dealt with evaluation of text material. "How to Pick a Topic" and "The Main Idea" lessons were the most difficult for them. The problem of determining the main idea surfaced again in "The Parts of the Book" lesson (the worksheet sets for these three lessons appear in appendix 3) and in the final meetings, when students were to take notes on the key issues in assigned articles as one of the steps in collecting and organizing information for a research paper. This problem was also dealt with in the English instruction, but the library, with its extensive primary sources and tools for evaluative functions (e.g., digests and synopses), served as practical reinforcement for the abstract discussions in the classrooms. On the other hand, the value of the relatively brief library sessions was largely established by the background instruction provided by the classroom teaching and the students' resultant needs.

Chiefly, there was a need for flexibility in library instruction in order to meet unexpected needs of the students, to shorten assignments that unexpectedly proved troublesome, to capitalize on unanticipated enthusiasm, etc. The tutorial potential in the students was an unlooked for asset that was particularly useful throughout both semesters.

Besides a constant reinforcing of the importance of information handling to their academic and future success, a concentrated effort was made throughout the library input—both in development of the material and in conducting the instructional periods—to highlight the "excitement" of information; for example, information gathering, evaluation, and organization were often linked to the processes a detective or a lawyer must follow to solve a mystery or win a case. Here again, the ability to be flexible so as to respond to the developing interest of students in information handling and library tools was most important.

In addition every appropriate opportunity was taken to introduce enjoyment into the work. For example, the introductory session for the card catalog consisted of an hour of "card" playing. Each student was supplied with a minicard catalog of thirty-two cards, grouped by books, which were reorganized to match the Brooklyn College library's split catalog arrangement. Even lollipops were used. In the assignment on "parts of the book," students were asked to "discover" the author's reasons for proposing that tiny children should learn to read from simply reading the table of contents.[2] Four of the five reasons are clearly given, but the fifth called for an inference from "Who Has Trouble, the Reader or the Non-reader?" to "Non-readers Have Trouble in School." Given the students' difficulty in making content evaluations, this was an anticipated difficulty, and, in fact, only one student in each semester "discovered" this reason. However, all the students were delighted when a classmate was presented the lollipop, which had been "jokingly" mentioned the week previously, as the reward for work "up and beyond" what was expected of them.

The final class session in both semesters for the weekly experimental groups featured a treasure hunt, followed by coffee and refreshments. The treasure hunt was designed (instead of an examination) to review the key resources in the library. Seven clues, each leading to the next, were provided for each team. The first team which located all seven clues and returned to the room received the prize. The treasure hunt was designed not only to reinforce the library instruction but to add subconsciously to the students' feeling that the library could be an enjoyable place, as well as helpful to them. The English professors joined their classes on those days and the food arrangements were decided by the students—from Spanish coffee to a smuggled-in bottle of wine. The relaxed party atmosphere provided the opportunity for candid feedback from the students regarding the course.

These were modest efforts, but they constituted a thread of responsive flexibility that ran throughout the course for attracting and fostering the intellectual growth of young people who came from families in which no one had previously attended college.

Statistical Results

The stage was set and the play went on for two semesters. What did we have at curtain call? Quite a bit, in differing magnitudes. As had been decided, the experiment was to be judged on measurable results: Could the library-based instruction be shown to have had an effect in the academic success of the students? This basis for judgment was necessary for several reasons. It could be measured, and, being of prime importance both to administrators and the teaching faculty, it was the point on which future action (adoption of further programs of library-based instruction) would be determined. It was also essential that concrete, measurable results should be achieved so that librarians would know whether this was, in fact, one of the ways in which library resources, both materials and personnel, could significantly help in this tremendous educational undertaking or whether another route should be tried.

The results (which follow) start with primary concerns and then highlight some considerations that were barely touched upon in this study, which we hope other academic librarians will investigate further. Another set of results is of a more immediate and people-related concern; that is, how the people involved with the experiment responded and how the responses affected what happened at Brooklyn College in subsequent semesters.

The results of the experiment contained some surprises. Comparing the before and after papers of all the groups—that is, subtracting the grade (obtained by averaging the five numerical grades assigned each paper by the outside graders) for each student's initial paper from the grade received on the final paper—disclosed a mean gain of 11.65 for students who received the weekly instruction, 5.51 for students who received the traditional library instruction, and 11.18 for the students in the control groups. By a similar method of comparison, the weekly instructed groups improved by an average of 23 percent, the traditionally instructed groups by 10.11 percent, and the control groups by 20.25 percent.

The weekly library instruction produced the highest academic gain, as evidenced by the best improvement in ability to produce a research paper defending a chosen proposition over a semester's time. Despite the fact that the difference between the weekly and control groupings is modest, it is worthy of most careful study, as only an unaccountable fluke kept these results from being statistically significant. Analysis of the mean point gains and percentages of improvement for the various English 1.2 sections disclosed that one weekly instructed group had the highest (19.05) and the other the lowest (4.24) mean point gain. The cause lies, to large degree, in the fact that the latter group had the highest mean grade on the initial paper, 74.4 (see appendix 2), which meant that there was considerably less room for improvement than in any other section. While there was not a direct correlation to support this point as the responsible factor, there was supportive evidence if one compared the mean grades on the initial papers in other groups.

Replications of this experiment or similar studies could easily substantiate or disprove this hypothesis. Should it be proved, the results of this study would carry even greater weight for the potential of library-based instruction in the academic success of students, as a comparable mean point gain in the second weekly group would have thrown the positive results far into the significant range and made the percent of improvement between the weekly and the control groups over 53 percent.

The results of the experiment indicate that differences in library programs can have differing effects on students' academic performance. Indeed comparisons of mean grade point gains establish the pattern which continued almost without exception throughout the total consideration of the academic development of these three groupings: the weekly grouping ranking highest, followed by the control grouping, with the traditional grouping considerably lower. This pattern can be seen quite clearly in table 1, which shows the rank ordering of student progress by English sections for the seven key areas explored in terms of academic success.

While the rank orders of student progress in the indicated areas showed a very mixed situation, the summary of these ranks by type of library input showed the same relationship between the experimental groupings as the mean gain and percentage of improvement comparisons did; that is, the groups that received the weekly library instruction ranked first, with a group average of 22; the groups that received the traditional library instruction ranked lowest, with a group average of 30.5; and the control groups averaged 27.75. Here, however, the control groupings fell closer to the ranking of the traditional group than to the weekly instructed group.

This pattern was broken in an extremely crucial area, student retention. In this case, both library inputs achieved better results than those achieved by the control group. The percentages of students who completed the English course requirements were as follows: 79 percent of the students with weekly library instruction, 70 percent of the students who received the traditional library input, and 64 percent of the students in the control groups. Since a frequent pattern for educationally disadvantaged students is to at-

TABLE 1
Rank Order of Student Progress

Group[1]	Point Gain between Papers	% Improvement between Papers	% Completed Course Requirements	Passed Course	Completed Following Semester with Credit	Increase in Number of Tools Used	Number of Tools Used by Semester End	Total
ASW	1	1	4	4	4	4	2	20
ASC	2	2	7	6	7	1	4	29
BST	5	4	5	1	3	6	3	27
BSC	3	3	3	5	6	6	1	27
BFW	7	7	2	1	2	3	2	24
BFC	4	5	1	1	1	2	3	17
AFT	8	8	2	3	5	5	3	34
AFC	6	6	6	2	8	7	3	38

Note: For clarity, this rank ordering assigns the same whole-number rank to groups that placed at the same level.

[1]A/B = Designation for Professors
S/F = Semester Designation
W = Weekly Instruction
T = Traditional Instruction
C = Control Group

tend at the beginning of the semester and then drop out, any academic experience which, like the library-based instruction in general and the weekly library input in particular, promotes student detention is of major importance. The retention potential of the library-based instruction was confirmed by the percentages of students from the three experimental groupings which completed course work with credit for the semester following the one in which they were involved in the experiment: 77 percent of the weekly instructed students successfully completed course work the following semester, as did 71 percent of the traditionally instructed students and 68.75 of the control students.

The students in the remedial Q sections represented a homogeneous grouping in writing ability, as determined by the English placement exam, and since the variance between the high school averages for the three experimental groupings was little more than 2 percent (71.01 for students receiving the weekly instruction, 71.26 for students receiving the traditional instruction, 72.30 for students in the control groups), it is obvious that differences in the performance of the groups could not be attributed to differences in students' initial academic abilities from one group to another. Therefore, before we leave the primary evaluative concerns of this study, it should be stated again that the experiment demonstrated that correlated library and information retrieval assistance which emphasizes information collection skills and facility in the evaluation of resources in relation to a remedial writing course clearly contributed to the retention rate of students and, to some degree, facilitated the students' academic success in the course.

Yet at the same time that the weekly instruction was contributing to the academic success of educationally disadvantaged students in the English course, the traditional library instruction not only did not promote the academic success of the students, it netted less favorable results than no library instruction at all. This turned out to be the most surprising and perhaps most important finding of the study.

The relationship proved statistically significant when testing whether the type of library input or lack of it is related to performance in the course, where improvement is indicated by improvement or no improvement in the grade received on the second paper as compared to the first. According to the criterion value of chi square, $(r - 1)(c - 1) = 1$ degree of freedom, the 0.05 level of significance was 3.841 and the traditional/control results tested at 4.64. (The traditional/weekly results tested at 3.71 and so still fell within the range of chance, as was the case with the weekly/control results.) Of all the results, this one is of most immediate concern to the profession, as this traditionally limited input of library instruction is the one most frequently employed in academic libraries.

When the statistics are regrouped, some secondary conclusions present themselves. As has been mentioned, the differences in the two professors' approaches had an immense effect on the groups, and a study of the achievements of the professors' classes clearly indicated that the winning combination, so far as the academic success of basic-skills freshmen was concerned, was the demanding, unsympathetic Professor A, with the weekly library instruction. The only point at which his section (receiving the weekly library input) was topped was in the percentage of students who completed the English 1.2 course; it was at this point that Professor B's nurturing had more effect than the library input. However, the positive effect of the library input in the retention rate among Professor A's group was unquestionable, both in regard to the English 1.2 course and these students' academic performance the following semester.

The basic pattern of the weekly grouping ranking first followed by the control grouping and then by the traditional, with one exception, held true as to the stated use of the library and library resources as indicated on the IBM questionnaire cards completed by the students during the first and final weeks of class and indicated in table 2. (The use of library tools is presented as stated by the students and was not verified.) These data presented a particular problem in interpretation, because of the effect caused by the variance in the number of students in each group; that is, by necessity, those who were included had to have completed both cards. For example, the percentages of gain in the average number of different uses made of the library during the semester of the experiment is highest for Professor A's spring control group; however, since only four sets of cards were obtainable for this group, the results unduly slant the overall results in favor of the control groups. Thus while overall the weekly instructed group ranks highest in percentage of gain in variety of use, the control group, it can be safely surmised, would not have been so close a second had the majority of students in Professor A's control class not dropped out by the end of the semester.

Again, the groups that received the weekly library instruction ranked highest in all three use categories. The groups that received the traditional library instruction moved into second place only in the number of different purposes for which the students used the library by the end of the semester they were involved in the experiment.

The traditional groups moved out of last place only one other time: in the mean grade-point average gain between the semester of the experiment and the following semester. The weekly library instruction groups had $+0.35$, the traditional groups $+0.23$, and the control groups $+0.01$. The mean dropout rate of students between the two semesters was three for both the weekly library instruction and control groups, with the traditional groups at four.

TABLE 2

Student Use of Library and Library Tools

Average Number of Different Uses Made of Library during Semesters		Percent of Gain in Variety of Use over Semesters		Percent of Gain in Library Use over Semesters	
W	10.0	W	33	W	43
T	9.4	T	31.5	C	42
C	8.9	C	24	T	28

W = Weekly Instruction   T = Traditional Instruction
C = Control Group

Thus while the weekly instruction had a positive effect on students' academic success and their use of the library and its resources, the traditional library input (i.e., a library tour plus lectures on the card catalog and the *Reader's Guide*) had in most cases, in comparison to the control grouping, a negative effect on the same issues. The "why" of this result is material for another study, but the ill effects from some (but insufficient) library instruction have already been raised in library literature, for example, the general dissatisfaction with one-shot instructional efforts as library orientation tours.

An analysis of student performance by sex showed that, despite a high school average less than two points higher, the male students in the experiment performed better than the female students in everything but passing the English 1.2 course. An analysis of the data as they relate to the sex of the students also showed that Professor A, a male, retained 66 percent of the males in his sections and 58 percent of the females, and, with the exception of his assignment of passing grades, the males in his sections did consistently better in the areas cited. Professor B, a female, retained 75 percent of the males enrolled in her sections and 91 percent of the females, and the relative success between the sexes in her groups varied from area to area and group to group. Whether such differences are due to the sex of the professors and/or the students, as opposed to the contrasting teaching modes of the professors, is open to question.

A study of the rank composite list of high school averages revealed no relationship between a student's high school average and his point gain or percent improvement. Dividing the 110 scores into fifths shows that six students in the highest fifth and ten students in the second fifth received point gains over 10; there were nine students in the third fifth, eleven in the fourth fifth, and three in the lowest fifth. Conversely, in the highest fifth, three students had negative point gains; in the second fifth there were no negative point gains; in the third fifth, two had negative point gains; and one in the fourth and two in the lowest fifth. Of the students who did not have gain points recorded because they did not complete their second paper, four were in the highest fifth, seven in the second fifth, six in the third fifth, six in the fourth fifth, and eight in the lowest fifth. This again pointed out the difficulty of estimating student potential for academic success on the basis of prior performance evaluations and brings us full cycle in consideration of these particular students' abilities.

People-related Results

If the former results—those that could be transformed into statistics to substantiate the role of the librarian as a partner in the education process with "outsiders" (i.e., faculty and administrators)—are needed to pave the way for respectable library-based instruction, the people-related results certainly provide a valid secondary rationale for establishing such programs.

Librarians often find that the concept of library instruction is welcomed. Putting it into practice, however, is resisted because that takes time and money. Consequently, rather than risk censure of their instructional activities, librarians often undertake new instructional efforts in the least conspicuous manner possible. A case in point occurred at Brooklyn College.

When the proposal for the experiment was first presented to the Department of Educational Services, the chairman and his second-in-command were most enthusiastic about the opportunity and promised all the support necessary (e.g., access to student records and special scheduling arrangements). The third-in-command, however, was quite outspoken about his lack of enthusiasm and pointedly asked me: "What are you going to get out of this?" Less than a year later, when the experiment got under way, the head of the department had been promoted and his second-in-command had retired due to ill health, creating a very precarious situation for the experiment since the third-in-command was now in charge.

Every effort was made, therefore, to be as invisible as possible and direct contact with the Department of Educational Services was handled through the librarian on line to the department. Halfway into the spring semester, a terse note from the chairman requested a report on the experiment, but there was no response when the report was subsequently submitted. About this time, a meeting of the faculty of the Department of Educational Services was called to discuss ways of providing improved academic support for their students. That evening, Professor A called me at home and said, "For heaven's sake, why doesn't the chairman know what you are doing?

Half the ideas they brought up at the department meeting today, I had to tell how you were already doing them. You should get your materials to the chairman; he's really interested in what you are doing."

After the chairman received the library-based instruction program material, the results to date were discussed with him. The chairman said that he had to deal with 5,000 students and could not give them all that the weekly program provided. Based on the results of the experiments, however, he concluded that he could give *something* extra to more of them and he asked what I would suggest. Eventually he decided to add two more librarians to his staff for the following fall and approved the planning for a series of videotapes to provide basic informational concepts to all DES students in conjunction with the remedial writing course.

Administrative interest in the library program was also expressed in an invitation to formally recruit students into the profession. An administrator in the Department of Educational Services asked me to address a group of educationally disadvantaged students on librarianship as a career. Interest in the topic was clearly evident throughout the informal discussion, but it was also evident that not one of them had ever before considered a library career.

Perhaps it should be emphasized that the initial interest and belief of the administrators in the value of the library instruction was not promoted by either the DES librarian or me, because both of us tried to be as inconspicuous as possible in relation to the experiment. The program was promoted through the very enthusiastic actions of a faculty member who saw his students benefiting from the library enrichment. Another professor, who after the class lecture on the card catalog had confessed, "I'm ashamed to tell you that I didn't know a lot of this," was an effective promoter of the library program with her colleagues.

In retrospect, it is obvious that the attempt to keep a low profile was not a good policy. There are, in fact, two very real dangers in such an approach to the politics of library instruction. First, it limits the resources that can be utilized in support of the learning experience and the amount of student involvement—both of which are crucial to the success of any library instruction program. Second, should the program succeed, as did the Brooklyn College experiment, the administrators may well resent not being informed of activities under their jurisdiction and not being able to share the credit for the success. A far better approach—though not without danger—is to state clearly the instructional objectives and to assume responsibility publicly for their achievement. Faculty and administrative cooperation is crucial to every library-instruction program.

The greatest reward came from the response of the students. As previously discussed, the two classes varied considerably in their interclass relationships and their conception of my relation to the professor and the course. A few students had almost insurmountable educational difficulties, but the general enthusiasm and appreciation of the students for their growing confidence in informational activities was most heartwarming. As their fears abated and their self-confidence in using the library and its resources grew, many of them began to enjoy their library experiences.

Previous work with SEEK students at Queens College had in general elicited a "very happy" response to library training, even with those who complained at first,[3] and at UCLA, where self-directed library instruction units were prepared for disadvantaged Chicano students, "the main difficulty came when the students, enjoying the game, demanded to have more than three units a week, and threatened to outrun the frantic preparation of teaching assistants and librarians."[4] Therefore, as student enjoyment was one of the aims of the library-based instruction and since disadvantaged students' capacity for such enjoyment had already been attested to in library literature, it did not come as a great surprise—but it came as a great satisfaction.

At Brooklyn College, students from both sections that received the weekly library instruction indicated a failure in their previous school experiences to give them even an elementary exposure to the information potential of the libraries; both groups showed excitement at various times during the course over the richness of the materials and information available in the library. Regular attendants gained confidence in the library over the semester, which was clearly evidenced in the difference in which they reacted to the library on the tours at the outset of the semesters—in most cases with a blend of meekness and hostility—and the enthusiasm with which they raced through the library during the last sessions' "treasure hunts."

How much student self-confidence and enjoyment in use of the library influenced some of the statistical outcome cannot be known. However, there is no question that students in the groupings receiving weekly instruction had a better retention record in the completion of course requirements than did the students in either of the other groups. This retention record is of crucial importance as it represents the counteraction of the normal pattern of rapid dropout among disadvantaged students, an end which remedial programs often are designed to meet.[5] Where the English-class atmosphere was less conducive for student self-confidence and enjoyment of learning (i.e., Professor A's section), the importance of the library instruction became even more important in fostering such attitudes.

Criticisms were elicited from both of the weekly instructed groups, but the only criticisms that could be obtained from Professor B's class were that a week was too far apart for the meetings in the library, as the students tended to forget too much between sessions, and that they needed the course (both the writing and information skills) sooner, or concentrated early in the semester, because the skills were also important for their other courses that required term papers.

The following dialogue occurred in Professor A's class, which received weekly instruction, one day when students complained about the lack of instruction in writing and research training in their earlier schooling.

Student A: This kind of learning should be exploited in junior high school and in high school.

Librarian: I agree with this. For instance, with library things, I think children should start learning in first grade . . .

Student A: [Interrupting] I didn't even know there existed a *Reader's Guide to Periodical Literature.* I didn't know there were books with quotations. I didn't know there were summaries of books 600 pages long made in two paragraphs. I didn't know this.

Student B: I didn't know there is a book for everything: whatever you want to look for, short stories or quotations.

Student A: I only knew there was one type of dictionary. I didn't know there were psychology dictionaries, sociology dictionaries. Look in the dictionary—Websters, Websters. Everywhere and everything is Websters. But if you are doing a course in history there could be a historical dictionary.

Librarian: There is.

Student A: There is! I didn't know this.

Student B: I thought I didn't know it because I didn't go to high school. I only have eighth grade. But now you went to high school and then you say you didn't even know it.

Student A: You'd be surprised! You'd be surprised!

With a little effort, "stuffy" libraries can turn students on! The student who evidenced the greatest improvement between her papers was a young black woman in Professor A's weekly group. Starting with a paper with a mean score of 36, she finished the course with a paper that earned a mean score of 80, for 122 percent improvement. This student's high school average was 66.73, compared to 71.79, the mean for all groups. She was not particularly outstanding in any way except that she epitomized the excitement that many students began to feel for the process of information handling. When she began her final class paper, she determined "to use one of every kind of source." Unfortunately, her topic, "Males as Teachers," made her task difficult, but it led her to use the *Education Index,* a tool that was not covered in the library-based instruction. This student exemplified one of the most satisfying aspects of the experiment: not only is it possible for students to learn library-based skills with a certain amount of enjoyment, the enjoyment can be transferred to the learning process.

A 1972 figure from the Bureau of Libraries stated that only 2 percent of professional librarians were from minority groups, and a major concern of the library profession for the past several years, as evidenced by the Illinois Manpower Project, has been the recruitment of minority personnel into its ranks. This problem might be partially solved by adequate library instruction, such as weekly experimental sessions provided. Before the experiment, a library career had never crossed the mind of any of these students, but during both semesters students inquired about librarianship as a career. One of the girls even got herself a position in the library on a work-study program the semester after her participation in the experiment. It is impossible to speculate on how many of these students will eventually enter the field, particularly since they were freshmen, but at least the idea has been implanted.

Part of their interest in the profession may reflect a changing concept of "the librarian." During the first semester of the experiment, the English discussion had centered around stereotypes, and on the way to the library instruction afterward, the stereotype of the librarian was discussed: the little old lady with glasses. To which a student added: "Yea, who sits behind a desk and pushes a lot of papers around!" By the end of the semester, and after rather extensive exposure to both the DES librarian and me, the students had new images for their concept of "the librarian." With the department's subsequent employment of additional librarians to work specifically with educationally disadvantaged students, this concept would become even more well rounded and would reinforce the positive feelings students had about the library-based instruction and the library itself. Most importantly, some of the students would still be in college—and able to meet the new, real librarians—because of, and only because of, the library-based instruction they had received.

CHAPTER NINE

Roadmarks and Roadblocks

●

●

What conclusions can be reached from the two-semester study done at Brooklyn College with disadvantaged freshmen and in what directions do they point? Certainly the statistics and the responses of the students, faculty, and administrators all point to the fact that the weekly program of correlated library and information retrieval assistance can contribute to the academic success of disadvantaged college freshmen and to student use of the library. There is also indication that the answer to disadvantaged college freshmen's academic needs lies not in less demanding work but in adequate support programs, in which library-based instruction can play a significant role.

The very negative results of the traditional library approach, that is, a library tour and lectures in how to use key library tools, are a most serious outcome, which should be further explored. (It's so serious that, as a careful reader will have observed, it was impossible not to raise the warning flags prior to this.) Libraries whose instructional programs consist exclusively or primarily of orientation tours (and perhaps lectures on the card catalog and/or the *Reader's Guide*) can no longer afford to ignore the very real fact that their efforts may be turning students "off" the library. The negative showing of the traditional approach in combination with the results of the weekly instruction substantiates a fact already attested to in library literature: library instruction must be closely related to students' immediate classroom needs.

The very poor showing of the traditional instruction may also support the feeling of many educators involved with disadvantaged students that students' self-esteem and self-confidence have a direct correlation with their academic success. It may well be that exposure to libraries and library resources without sufficient skill development may be an overwhelming experience that intimidates students and therefore creates negative feelings toward the library. This would be in direct contrast to the response of students who had sufficient exposure to the library and its tools to become enthusiastic over their use, as was evidenced in the dialogue in the previous chapter.

Previously, it may have been all but impossible to arrange an adequate amount of students' time to ensure effective programs of library instruction, but there is an obvious openness to experimentation within most programs and departments involved with remedial academic endeavors. As part of the faculty members' self-evaluation, and with their concern for open admissions students' not just getting information but also for helping them take that information and assimilate it, turn it around, and think about it, some faculty members can for the first time really value the librarian as a partner in the educational program. How easy it is for faculty in general to accept this concept may well depend on the ability of librarians to adopt and convincingly enunciate the faculty's concept that the library's value is in supporting the achievement of the faculty's teaching objectives. That the library, which is often regarded with apathy by faculty and administrators, can under these circumstances find a more positive response is evidenced not only by this experiment put by the work that was being done elsewhere in CUNY libraries (as cited earlier in this book). The enthusiasm of the parties involved with the experiment certainly did much in raising the esteem and appreciation for libraries and librarians on the Brooklyn College campus, and there is no reason to believe that such support would not be forthcoming on other campuses as well.

This experiment, moreover, and perhaps most importantly, shows that it is possible to evaluate the library's contribution to the educational function of its institution in statistical terms which are meaningful to students, faculty, and administrators. Certainly other controlled experiments are called for, not only to replicate this study but to establish the value of many other library instructional activities.

There are, of course, great difficulties in such experiments, particularly as was anticipated in determining a valid way to measure academic achievement. It would be of value for someone in the Department of Educational Services or the Brooklyn College library to do a follow-up study on the students approximately four or five years after the experiment to see which students completed their studies and what they did after graduation. This would seem to be the most valid measurement of academic success, but since there are many extenuating circumstances, such as lack of funds (which might in the long run be the deciding factor in a student's completion of his academic program), if such a study is conducted it would be necessary to determine why students did not finish the undergraduate program. An in-depth study of only a few of these students might provide invaluable insights into the role of library instruction in the academic performance of disadvantaged students.[1]

Another conclusion is that information and libraries can be exciting to students. The exact rationale behind this may be hard to determine; however, adequate library instruction answers three of the chief needs of the disadvantaged student as outlined by educators: it makes possible the individualization of the student's program; it enhances self-confidence and self-esteem as the student gains mastery over information tools; and it allows the student to relate studies to topics and projects that are meaningful and relate to the real-life situation.

The experiment, if the interest expressed by students in the weekly instruction is any indication of their true state of mind, also indicates that one does not have to be a member of a minority group or come from a disadvantaged background to communicate with these students, though it may call for cultivating capacity to learn from the students on the part of instructors and librarians.[2] This is of particular importance since many librarians are openly concerned about their ability to relate to students of racial or ethnic backgrounds different from their own.[3] Moreover, satisfying experiences of library instruction provide a recruitment base for the profession among seldom-reached groups.

Just as an ongoing flexibility was necessary in offering the library-based instruction, both to keep it closely synchronized with the English course and to capitalize on such unforeseen opportunities as peer tutoring, flexibility is required in the total library instruction program for disadvantaged students.[4] Learning by the disadvantaged is still largely an uncharted endeavor, and only by experimenting with approaches and techniques and carefully eliciting feed back from the students can optimal experiences be designed. The only thing that is certain about such program planning is that the answer will always be a multiple approach, which will reflect the individualized needs of students and which will constantly evolve.

A good example of this need for flexibility can be seen in the activities of the three librarians on line to the Department of Educational Services at Brooklyn College the year following the experiment. The original DES librarian, Bernice Martin, worked with the experiment from its planning stages through its implementation, and since then has adapted many of the techniques and materials developed for the experiment into her regular assignments. Professor Martin has an office in the Brooklyn College library and maintains regular office hours, when DES students can come to her for individual help on research problems. She also goes into classrooms, upon request, to give lectures (usually in connection with assignment of a research paper) and conducts workshops in research skills for small groups of students (usually five to seven a semester) upon request. During the fall and spring of 1972/73, for example, she gave approximately two dozen classroom lectures and conducted half a dozen workshops.

Two other librarians were employed by the Department of Educational Services in the fall of 1972. One worked in the library of Brooklyn College's downtown campus, and her activities paralleled those of Professor Martin. During the same period, she gave three classroom lectures and conducted six workshops. The third librarian was assigned to the Reading and Study Skills Center, where she provides individual tutoring in research skills and reading. Requests for workshops in research skills normally go to the center, and this librarian presented forty-one workshops, classroom lectures, and library tours during the 1972-73 academic year.

These three librarians coordinated their efforts in planning the content for the lectures and workshops. They found an ongoing need for evaluation and planning.

Professor Martin was asked to provide a research skills component in a summer Head Start program for incoming DES students in 1972. Classes averaged twelve students, and six of them met with Professor Martin twice a week for one-hour sessions during the five-week program. At the end of the program the students were asked to complete questionnaires on the value of the different components of the program. The returns were light but the research skills component received the highest rating, and on the basis of this the director of the summer program doubled the librarian input the following summer. Some of the written comments of students on the questionnaire follow.

> Helped students to learn how to use B.C. library.
> It showed us where and how to find various information.
> Our guide through the library was a nice person.
> We were shown how to get all the information the college had to offer. This prevented confusion in September for me.
> The use of the library was extremely helpful to me.
> I don't think anything could of been improved.
> Stress this. The best thing you could have done was this. I got a B in English because I knew how to use the library.
> This was very useful for me.
> This part was great, though it would be even more helpful if continued during the Freshmen semester at B'klyn College.

Should be part of the course offered at Brooklyn College. This was
most helpful in learning about the library and in finding the different
kinds of material the library offers. No complaint.

The need for flexibility in serving disadvantaged students is supported by
both the experiment and the expansion of the library services offered by the
Department of Educational Services after the experiment. Certainly, a variety of teaching methods is available for library-based instruction and the
methods are worthy of careful consideration.[5]

Another conclusion which can happily be drawn is that, though there is
little in the literature about library services to the disadvantaged *per se,*
there is literature which can help: on library instruction (much of which
was referred to in chapter 6) and remedial collegiate programs (most of
which are available through ERIC). One would best begin with the literature
describing the types of programs and services which have proved most
successful with the academically disadvantaged and distinguish the common
elements which could relate to the learning of information handling skills.
Then one can proceed to the most promising or documented forms of library
instruction and select those which offer the desired elements and are feasible
for a particular campus. In every case librarians will have to make their
own applications and design their own programs to meet the particular
needs of their campus, for there is no clear-cut path to follow; indeed, there
are many good paths to explore.

The fact remains, however, that the lack of literature on library programs
for the disadvantaged points to a lack of effort in this critical area. A study
of academic libraries' responses to new directions in undergraduate education concludes: "there is little reexamination of purposes or reordering of
priorities."[6] This study found that most academic libraries simply coped
with pressures as they become critical. Independent study demands more
involvement with the library staff and more depth in library holdings, as
well as more instruction for students in the use of libraries. Yet there is
little evidence of change in these areas. The study of CUNY libraries in the
first fall of open admissions (cited in chapter 3) showed that there, too, little
new work was being done in preparation for one of the major educational
developments of our lifetime.

This situation, plus the outcome of the experiment, leads to the final conclusion: More research, experimentation, evaluation, and information dissemination are needed regarding the educational function of libraries in the
academic program of disadvantaged students.

Each current or anticipated instruction-related library program should be
carefully analyzed for its relationship to the literature and existing practices.
The programs should be established with a view to measurable outcomes so

that meaningful evaluation can be assured, and each undertaking should be considered experimental until its worth is proved. Descriptions and evaluation results of successful and unsuccessful programs should be made available as a matter of course to the profession at large.

Given the demands upon most academic libraries today, it seems almost unfair that librarians, who already extend their services to provide new instructional services to meet educationally disadvantaged student needs, should also bear the burden of stringent evaluation procedures and dissemination of successes—much less failures. These added responsibilities, however, are essential to establish the validity of the library's educational role on campus and to help make the profession's response to students' academic needs more effective. We need to strengthen and support each other's efforts in the particular, so that academic librarianship may assume its proper position as an essential element in achieving the educational goals of higher education in meeting the needs of disadvantaged students.

The primary roadblock to reaching this goal was presented in chapter 3: an attitudinal matter among librarians. For such avenues of service to be opened, the unity and commitment of academic library staffs are required. It must be a commitment of vision and muscle. It must be a commitment that will lead to a reordering of priorities within the present resources, staff, and financial boundaries. Hard as it may seem, there will be no laurels, no rewards, until they are far along on their journey as full partners in the educational endeavors of their institutions.

CHAPTER TEN

Where Do We Go
from Here?

●

●

I am the mother of an 11-year-old boy, but by extension and a vivid imagination, I am the mother of all school-age children. And what I want for my children is the best education possible, an education that will prepare them not only for their needs of today but for lifelong professional and personal growth experiences. The trouble is, of course, that I know that they are not going to get it. What is being taught today is essentially—though watered down—the same educational bill of fare I was served, which is totally inadequate to meet the demands of this generation's societal and professional needs. If they are taught as I was, young people will be grossly out of date before they even accept their diplomas.

Moreover, my son has over the past two years relegated most of his school experiences to the category of the most boring work situations. At an earlier age, the boundaries between work, play, and learning were very blurred for him. Now what he looks forward to at school are his duties as a traffic patrol and milk monitor and the Mother's Day play, in which he has a part. Obviously, it is not work, in and of itself, that is distasteful to him.

We live in a period in which students of all ages, and their parents, have decided they have a right as consumers to a say in their own education,[1] and they are not satisfied with their educational opportunities. Thus student groups make demands for curriculum changes and individuals sue colleges; or we have—which is even more abhorrent to my way of thinking—student apathy.

If we did not know how to solve many of the educational problems facing us, it would be one thing; but we know: learner-centered education, with all that it implies—learning how to learn, multiple approaches to learning, learning at one's own pace, independent study, learning by discovery. Such activities can become reality only through a new and greatly expanded role for the library. If we need to throw out the terms "library," "librarian," and "library instruction," fine. But let's get on with the task.

Where do we, the librarians, go from here? How do we do our share in turning lip service into actuality? First, I think we have to own up to our share in the guilt. If, as discussed earlier in this book, open admissions is an exacerbation of problems already existing, the problems of academic libraries are not only related to open admissions but reflect a much deeper problem. We must accept the fact that our institutions are not perfect or ideal, and that nothing (as things now are) is sacred. Change is to be desired on an ongoing basis—not change for the sake of change but change for the sake of improvement. Because nothing else stays the same, the formal structures for education cannot stay the same.

Changes that are needed should not be dictated by open admissions students but by realization of the fact that although we are in the seventies, we are still operating very much as if we were in the twenties. Similar to this is the realization that such changes that are made in response to open admissions (i.e., the results of endeavors to meet the particular needs of educationally disadvantaged students) must be analyzed for their potential applications to the needs of all students. It may prove that serious efforts to educate the educationally disadvantaged student of today will entail such a radical rethinking of the educational process that we will have done something not just for him or her, but for all students. Let us accept open admissions as an impetus for reassessing our goals, priorities, and policies and for trying new methods of achieving them, to the end of more effective service, not only to the student who walks through our doors but to the student we have to lure through our doors.

This will require a greater flexibility or experimental spirit on the part of librarians. If many librarians have hesitated to break with tradition and try new service approaches, they have been even less willing to discipline themselves to critically evaluate old and new approaches and to admit failure where indicated. In medical research, scientists progress through a series of experiments, those which support and those which discredit their initial hypotheses. Librarians must acquire the same attitude.

After careful preliminary research, a hypothesis or service approach must be decided upon, and acted on, and the results evaluated on a predetermined schedule. Librarians do not fail when their hypothesis fails, they simply move on to a new hypothesis, a new service approach, and begin again— each time moving one step closer to the library's service goals.

What are those service goals for which we should be working? Ultimately there is only one: that every member of the academic community should be an effective user of information in all its forms. Once we talk about a particular academic setting, however, the long-range, impossible-to-reach goal takes on a more individual form, unique to its institution. What, for instance, is the population to be served? Student and faculty only, or does one include staff, members of the business or residential areas, or high school students? And what kind of students, with what kinds of needs, does one have: graduate as well as undergraduate, educationally prepared and/or disadvantaged, those right out of high school and/or those more mature, those who live on campus or commute, the liberal arts minded or those who pursue specific career objectives? The library instruction service, as the goal of a library, should be aligned with the educational goals of its institution and with the characteristics of the populations to be served.

Once an instructional or program goal is set at an academic institution, the normal procedure is to set about developing a curriculum plan to meet that goal. Certainly no college would decide to start a new program to prepare people for careers as paralegals and then, haphazardly, offer a workshop here, a tour of a law firm there. Yet isn't that precisely what academic libraries do by way of library instruction? I am convinced that, until librarians are willing to commit the time and effort necessary to design a total curriculum of library and information science for the consumers of information on their campus, no truly successful program of library-based instruction can emerge. It must be planned with the same concern and care as a curriculum for history or one of the sciences. It must be designed, even if it will be years before it is totally implemented or even if it seems unlikely that it will ever be totally implemented.

The steps in such curriculum planning are as follows:

1. *Identify groups to be served.* Start the planning process by considering the people to be served in appropriate groupings (e.g., community groups, staff, students, and faculty, with the latter two subdivided by departments and, if necessary, the students by level of academic preparedness).
2. *Define instructional needs.* Outline what information handling skills and knowledge are needed by each group to ensure that the individuals in them can locate and utilize appropriate resources.
3. *Develop learning matrix.* A matrix can be formed for an overall view of the library-based instructional needs of the institution (institutional size may require a series of matrices). Analysis of the matrix will permit a systematic (rather than the present haphazard) approach to library instructional offerings. It will reveal what needs are common throughout the campus, which demand a series of learning experiences rather than a one-time treatment, which instructional elements are prerequisites for others, etc.

4. *Set instructional priorities.* The relationships which emerge from the analysis of the matrix should be studied to determine the larger patterns of learning needs so that initial instructional priorities can be set accordingly. These priorities should be checked against the known concerns of students, faculty, and administrators for further refinement in their ranking.

5. *Determine administrative constraints.* Each priority area should be scrutinized in terms of administrative or cost considerations in terms of staff time and money. If, for example, in a large institution it was determined that everyone should be able to use five indexes, it should be obvious that individual or classroom instruction could not be the method selected. These approaches would require too much staff time, and neither could ensure that every student would have an opportunity to be instructed. However, although the development of good point-of-use tools for the five indexes would demand a heavy initial outlay of staff time and money, point-of-use tools would ultimately be time and cost efficient. It would also guarantee every student an opportunity to receive instruction in the use of all five indexes. In other words, close study of the learning matrix can largely determine what learning experiences are administratively feasible, given the size and complexity of the total learning group for a specific instructional priority.

6. *Set behavioral objectives.* By this point a program of library-based instruction for a campus will begin to emerge, showing various groupings of clientele around shared learning needs which can be met by one or more administratively acceptable instructional methods and for which priorities have been assigned. Within the designated high-priority areas (areas of priority may vary from year to year) behavioral objectives should be set. Indeed, it is most important that behavioral objectives be set before contents and methodology are determined. Only in this manner can the librarian know for sure whether he or she is succeeding, that is, whether the students are learning.

The setting of behavioral objectives may seem difficult at first, but the process is easily mastered. If, for example, all freshmen are scheduled into the library for one hour during orientation week, the first question to ask (in consultation with the learning matrix) is: What would you like students to *do* as a result of their contact with the library? Then start thinking in terms of what experiences will be required for the students to do it. (Approaching the situation from this point of reference would never, I believe, indicate the traditional orientation tour.)

7. *Determine contents and choose teaching methodology.* Exactly what will be covered, in what manner, to achieve the behavioral objective(s) for a particular instructional priority? In general terms, the best learning experiences are those which approximate real-life situations. From the example of the five indexes, this means that however good a teacher a librarian may be, no classroom experience has as high a learning potential as a point-of-use tool, which provides for the students' working through a search problem with one of the specified indexes in the reference area of the library. Moreover, as

opposed to classroom instruction, the point-of-use approach allows students who are competent with one or more indexes to skip over those learning experiences, rather than be "turned off" in boredom. In all cases an administratively acceptable method must be chosen which is also desirable on educational grounds.

8. *Evaluate.* Although evaluation is implied in the setting of behavioral objectives, it deserves emphasis. The first question is whether the learners can perform in the manner designated as the objective of the learning experience. If not, what went wrong? Should the learning experience be modified or discarded? If so, could the results be improved or could the activity be expanded to others or modified to meet related needs? Through evaluation, curriculum planning can be an ongoing procedure.

The process of designing a curriculum for library-based instruction is summarized in figure 1, but at this point many librarians probably think that this is all pie in the sky—that it can't work at their campus because they get students for only an hour during orientation week and (occasionally) when a professor asks them to teach something specific to a class. On the contrary, a carefully developed, written-out curriculum design can have three very positive applications for every campus:

1. It offers a clear-cut rationale for the size and scope of a quality program of library-based instruction for students, faculty, and administrators who don't comprehend the dimensions of the task of ensuring that students acquire adequate information handling skills.
2. It allows one to progress more efficiently toward the long-range goal. For example, it clarifies which priorities can be handled in-house and which require developing faculty or administrative support before proceeding, it helps one see how instructional packages, developed to meet the needs of one group, may be used for others.
3. When given a specific opportunity for library instruction, one can not only more easily determine the best use to make of that opportunity but can clearly delineate what one is covering and how it relates to the total needs of the students involved, both to their professor and to the students themselves. (The latter is particularly important, as far too often librarians try to crowd every bit of pertinent information into a designated time frame, a habit the Brooklyn College experiment and the literature have shown produces largely negative results.) A primary rule in library instruction should be: Carefully limit the amount of contents to be covered in order to ensure that students will not only be able to absorb the information but will be able to *do* something with what they have learned.

Only three learning approaches have been mentioned as examples, but there are many other possibilities which in a real-life situation should be con-

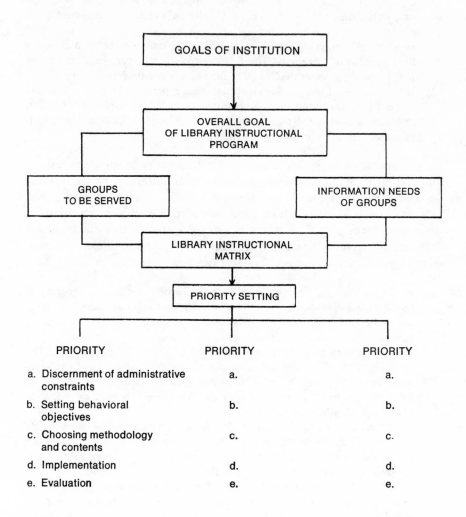

Figure 1. Developing a Curriculum of Library and Information Science for Consumers.

sidered, for besides flexibility, a diversity of approaches is needed in instructional programs. The discussion of new approaches in library instruction in this book and in the Brooklyn College experiment should not, therefore, be interpreted as indicating the best or only solutions to library instruction, much less to meeting the total needs of students, nor can they be if one remembers to start with an overall study of one's campus situation. Both in the library instruction sessions of the Brooklyn College experiment and in the patterns set by the librarians who were hired by the Department of Educational Services at the college there has been no more persistent concern than for flexibility and diversity.

In the years to come, librarians will have to explore—aggressively explore—many avenues of library-based instruction. To date, however, there has been a strong tendency—based most often, I believe, on the talents or predilections of the librarian(s) involved—to make a commitment to, and to develop, only one type of instructional program. This is not too different from the situation with the teaching faculty, but it is more obvious in the library program since it is the only one available to students, while there are many faculty among whom they may choose. The exception to this general trend is the multifaceted program at Sangamon State University (which was discussed on pages 35–36). Indeed, the diversity of the program (and the librarians' obvious ability to be flexible and responsive to the changing needs of the university) may largely account for its being, to date, the most ambitious and most successful foray by a library into the mainstream of higher education.

The need for diversity follows from the diversity of the students. There is not one instructional method or set of methods that is good for all people. Some educators are beginning to suspect that research on teaching effectiveness has been inconclusive and disappointing because the wrong questions are being asked. For the mythical statistical *average* student, it seems to make little difference what method is used, but when the data are examined student by student, it is clear that some students improve, some are unaffected, and some regress under various learning methods. "The very process of averaging the pluses, the minuses, and the nonchangers wipes out the message that different methods work for different students."[2]

Moreover, once librarians have practice in structuring their own programs for multiple approaches to learning, they will be in a better position to offer service to faculties that seek to diversify their courses through a wider use of resources and materials and/or to provide opportunities for programmed independent study (a method slowly but surely gaining momentum).[3] The value of such a learning environment will not accrue solely to the students but to society as a whole. At a time when many fear their demise,[4] the pluralism and diversity which are a part of our country's cherished heritage can be perpetuated through learner-centered education, made possible by librarians who are prepared to work in a partnership or leadership relation with faculty from the various disciplines.

The major deterrent to selecting one or more learning approaches to meet specific learning needs (as opposed to the general trend of picking a method of library instruction with which to work) is, I believe, the lack of educational skills. I'm afraid that, most often, instead of being pacesetters in the creative use of information in all its forms (as we often tell faculty they should be), we fall into the same poor habits of relying on lectures and bibliographies or other printed materials. Commitment to the educational function of libraries will necessitate, for most of us, a corollary commitment to continuing education; and libraries will need to provide in-house training for their professional staffs and/or opportunities for them to participate in courses and institutes where they can obtain expertise in teaching methodologies and media utilization. Perhaps, for political reasons, if no other, credentials equivalent to those of the teaching faculty (e.g., doctorates) will eventually be required in order to gain our distinct but equal standing as partners in higher education. The qualifications for the divisional librarian positions at Swarthmore, for example, call for "a doctor's degree in a relevant subject field, a library degree, and experience both in classroom teaching and library work."[5]

But let us go back to library instruction as it relates to open admissions. In the case of developing remedial programs (actually, in the development of all new academic goals and programs), librarians should not be passive until they are established. Rather, the library should take a more aggressive role in planning such programs on their campuses—those conducted during the academic year and those conducted under special conditions (e.g., Headstart programs). After all, could there be a more logical involvement for librarians than in planning remedial study and research skills programs? Library literature tells us, among other examples, that at Grambling College of Louisiana the librarian and the head of the Department of Elementary Education headed a Task Force Team on Reading, whose job was to establish a communication and study skills center.[6]

Even if a librarian's expertise were only in resource selection and utilization, such knowledge should be crucial in designing and equipping the services of study skills centers, because the proper mixture of materials in appropriate media formats, matched to students' interests and abilities, can go a long way toward ensuring the success of such centers. Yet most librarians have much more to offer in the planning stages. Mary Watson Hymon, head librarian at Grambling, was perceived as one who "knows not only the curriculum [and the] teaching problems, but more decisively the learning patterns and problems of the students."[7]

Beyond participation in planning efforts, librarians will want to be involved with the evaluation of remedial programs of which they are a part. An initial though limited study of some of the first open admissions graduates from Brooklyn College would seem to indicate that the college's remedial services, other than counseling, are not used by a great percentage of the students.[8] The library would have to be concerned about the validity of such a study, for, if valid, it would call for a reassessment of its services to educationally disadvantaged students. Evaluation is always to be desired, but particularly when one is working in new areas and with new clientele.

Whatever desirable pattern emerges for the library's role in meeting the needs of disadvantaged students after planning and initial evaluation, it is the responsibility of librarians to let administrators and faculty understand the educational function librarians can fulfill. This is a difficult task at best. To appraise the library's potential and maximized role in reaching the educational objectives of its parent institution and to reach internal agreement on the desired role of the library is a Herculean task. But even after a total curriculum design is established and agreed upon, the changed and expanded library role must still be "sold" to the administrators, faculty, and students (most of whom didn't know what to do with the library in its old, comfortable role).

The variety of opportunities is extensive, and perhaps the most important thing is for the head librarian and/or the staff to be actively involved in their community in order to learn how the library can best serve the educational pursuits of its institution. To accomplish this, librarians must begin by developing a clear understanding of those elements of the academic world which will inevitably play an important part in the outcome of their efforts (i.e., where the power lies) and then determine to use this understanding as a positive contribution to the development of a campaign to achieve their goals.

Certainly, it will involve librarians' venturing into the academic community to a degree seldom contemplated previously. There have been suggestions for "floating" librarians, who would go into the academic community and act as liaisons between students, faculty, and the library. Certainly any new or high-risk programs must have the support of faculty and students— particularly students in the programs—if they are to succeed. Ideally, librarians should seek input from students and faculty concerning their recommendations for developing and improving programs. This is not a new concept; service organizations have long recognized the value of encouraging the people they serve to participate in decision making. This practice not only keeps the organization keyed to the ever-changing needs of its clients but fosters vital personal contacts between staff and clientele. Indeed, there seems to be some indication of a growing effort in libraries to involve students to a greater extent in planning programs and in giving service.

Once positive results are achieved, faculty and student support and enthusiasm for the role of the library and its program are one of the most effective ways of reaching the administration, as evidenced in the experiment and as amply testified to in professional literature. Lack of such support will contribute to the failure of academic libraries, particularly in times of tightening budgets.[9] Ultimately, the administration has to be not only reached but convinced of the new work role for librarians if programs are to be properly supported.

Yet more than faculty and student support is usually needed to obtain administrative backing. Before administrators are willing to support innovations—particularly those involving additional expenses—they rightly require evidence that the proposed changes are worth the trouble they cause.[10] This fact of life points to the need of securing information on successful library programs on other campuses and/or developing small experiments on one's own campus that can be handled without major upheavals or expenditures, that can be constructed so as to give evidence of what the library could do if adequate provisions were made.

In fact, the overriding concern which emerged from a 1970 symposium on the academic library user was the lack of information on the amount, variety, and value of library instruction.[11] A 1971 survey, which had eighty-one responses to 107 questionnaires, found that none of the respondents had structured their research to determine the effectiveness of library orientation and instruction programs, except when theses and dissertations were involved. Only a few reported they had done any testing at all.[12] Further research is urgently needed to prove the educational value of library-based education. In particular, controlled experimentation with the various instructional alternatives for particular groups and situations is needed.

For example, one of the techniques for expanding library instruction within limited financial means (which should be immediately explored in relation to disadvantaged students and students in general) is the use of peer tutors. In literature on open admissions, a common theme (which the experiment confirmed) is use of the students in tutoring capacities. There is evidence that students who are overcoming their handicaps are particularly apt in helping other students overcome theirs (not to mention the motivational value of students' seeing their peers in positions of authority, as well as the positive reinforcement the tutors derive from the situation.)[13] The literature on this approach indicates that wide availability of tutoring services is important, that response is best when tutoring is offered as a service rather than a requirement, that paying student tutors provides some measure of control over their activities, and that participation of students and faculty in tutoring is a promising vehicle for building community.[14]

A library might wish to set up its own tutorial programs, but basic-skills departments normally have established tutorial procedures in connection with their counseling services and/or through reading, writing, and research clinics. Indeed, the need for such research and instructional service centers to bring about improvement in remedial English is considered of high priority in the literature on open admissions.[15] If such centers are already established, it should be an easy matter for librarians to utilize these situations in offering their services. Students who work closely with and benefit from a librarian's or a library-trained student's tutoring in a skills clinic will be more likely to use the library later.

If librarians have been slow to engage in serious planning and evaluation of services for educationally disadvantaged students, there is some consolation in the fact that they do not lag far behind other educators in this regard. Across the nation, remedial programs were created without detailed knowledge of what was being done elsewhere,[16] and many educators have been honest in questioning how far and with what assurance they can proceed without information more reliable and valid than conferences and the literature to date have produced.[17] The challenge is the same throughout higher education: to subject present practices and programs to ruthless analysis (and give them up if necessary) in order to achieve the development of each student to his and her highest desired ability, and with the exclusion of nobody. This is undoubtedly the most far-reaching reform in higher education of the postwar period, and yet, to date, there have been remarkably few studies evaluating the results.

It is possible that there has been more research and experimentation in this area than has been reported, but without dissemination of the results of such endeavors, their value is lost to the profession and to the students who might have been eventually benefited. Once having accomplished and initially evaluated any step toward the goal of quality universal education, therefore, the library and/or the college should work for adequate publicity of their efforts and the successful programs they produced. Certainly there is need for a clearinghouse for such information within the library profession. Such a responsibility might well fall within the province of the American Library Association's newly formed Library Instruction Round Table.

One lesson which history has provided is very clear: libraries cannot continue without people, but people are very likely to find a way toward fulfillment of their information needs outside the framework of the library's operation and control.[18] This is not to say that college libraries or the services they offer should be eliminated; much of what is being done is absolutely necessary and useful. It means that academic librarians can no longer confuse resources with services. It means that they must do more than they did before.

Just as there are no clear-cut or final solutions to the problems of open admissions, the need for flexibility and diversity dictates that there can be no single designated role for academic libraries in open admissions situations. We have evidence, however, that library staffs that are committed to helping students achieve academic success can greatly contribute to answering those questions and solving those problems. To do so, they must assume their inherent responsibilities in reaching the educational goals of their parent institutions. As librarians assume increased responsibilities, the literature in library instruction and in work for disadvantaged students must be carefully examined for the lessons they have to offer. Eventually, however, each curriculum of library-based instruction must be locally designed to meet the particular needs of the institution's students.[19]

Five guidelines that academic libraries should follow in offering library services for disadvantaged students in undergraduate programs can be summarized as follows:

1. Librarians should be actively involved in campus affairs so that they may take part in decisions which affect opportunities for their services; they should elicit student and faculty input as part of their own decision-making process.
2. The constant aim for disadvantaged college students should be quality undergraduate work, after sufficient remedial support is provided.
3. Sufficient time should be secured from students' programs to ensure the transfer of information-related skills. All efforts should be related to immediate student needs.
4. Librarians should be extremely open and flexible in the approaches they take to library-based instruction; a number of approaches may be appropriate.
5. Research, experimentation, evaluation, and dissemination of results should be ongoing concerns.

The challenge of open admissions is before us, or no farther away than tomorrow. If the library is really an integral element in education, it must begin to function as such, and its commitment must be for the needs of all students, not just the few who are academically talented. This is not to say that the job will be easy. On the contrary, there are decades of tradition and mountains of faculty, administration, and student indifference between libraries and the rightful role they can play in meeting this educational challenge.

But if the scanty literature and the results of this limited experiment at Brooklyn College can serve as indicators, librarians have a strategic role to play and would be remiss if they do not pursue it.

The rewards are immediate for the librarian who is involved with educationally disadvantaged students. The rewards will be even greater, because of the opportunity of open admissions, as librarians begin to offer the services that have always been needed in undergraduate education. And, finally, there is the reward described so well by John C. Frantz, while executive chairman of the National Book Committee:

> What we have . . . is a tremendous opportunity not only to respond to demands that we are beginning to feel . . . but also to help those who have a vision of what the United States and the world can have. To help them reach that vision . . . the libraries have been far too quiescent and to some extent under-estimated in the role that they can play not only in lending continuity to life in the city or neighborhood but also in encouraging rational discourse and productive change rather than revolution. And also they can do much more overtly than they have up to now to help change values that we know are selfish or obsolete or both and help us altogether to move toward a better future.[20]

Appendixes

Questionnaire sent to chief librarians
City University of New York
November 1970

LIBRARY OPEN ENROLLMENT QUESTIONNAIRE -- _____

The term OPEN ENROLLMENT STUDENTS refers to all freshmen who entered
the City University this fall and assumes that a number of these have poor
academic backgrounds.

Please make replies directly on the questionnaire. Comments will be
welcomed and may be given at the end of the questionnaire. If a comment
pertains to a particular question, please note the question number with
the comment. Thank you.

1. Give the number of full-time day students in the following categories:

	entering freshmen (including SEEK)	SEEK freshmen	total enrollment (including SEEK)	total SEEK enrollment
fall '67				
'68				
'69				
'70				

What was the projected number of freshmen for this fall under the Master
Plan? _____

2. Over the previous year, what new or additional provisions were made
for the library by the college administration?

	professional lines	nonprofessional lines	funds	space	other
fall '67					
'68					
'69					
'70					

Questionnaire--Continued

3. Was the actual situation created by open enrollment in the library this fall:

 _____ less difficult than anticipated
 _____ about as difficult as anticipated
 _____ more difficult than anticipated

4. On a scale of 1 to 10 (1 - completely unprepared; 10 - completely prepared), how prepared was the library for open enrollment when school began in September? _____

5. Prior to this fall were any studies and/or plans made by the library to prepare for open enrollment? yes ___ no ___
Please attach a copy of the findings of such investigations or briefly outline the findings below. Where specific suggestions were made, check those which to some extent are presently being implemented.

6. Have there been any contacts between the library and the various departments of the college and/or SEEK representatives for the purpose of coordinating the library's response to open enrollment with theirs? yes ___ no ___
Who initiated these contacts?

 ___ the library
 ___ the departments/SEEK
 ___ both

7. Responsibility for the library's planning and carrying out of services to open enrollment students has been assigned to:

 ___ one person; his title: _____
 to whom is he responsible: ___ head librarian
 ___ head of reader services
 ___ other (specify) _____
 _____

 ___ a committee; number of members: _____
 to whom is it responsible: ___ head librarian
 ___ head of reader services
 ___ other (specify) _____
 _____

Questionnaire--Continued

___ other (specify) _____

___ such responsibility has not specifically been assigned

8. (a) Formal instruction currently received by freshmen in the use of the library and library materials consists of:

___ orientation tours   ___ classroom teaching
___ group lectures in the library   ___ other (specify) _____

(b) Who is responsible for taking the initiative in providing such instruction?

___ the students themselves   ___ the library
___ the faculty   ___ other (specify) _____

(c) Does every freshman receive some formal library instruction?
yes ___ no ___

(d) Are library handbooks available for freshmen? yes ___ no ___

9. Have changes been made in acquistions policies as a result of open enrollment? yes ___ no ___
Please state briefly the changes made or attach copies of directives issued on this subject.

10. In the past have nonprint materials been purchased on a regular basis for the collection? yes ___ no ___ Check types:

___ filmloops   ___ records
___ filmstrips   ___ tapes
___ other (specify) _____

Are nonprint materials being purchased specifically for freshmen (e.g., remedial, basic skills materials, etc.)? yes ___ no ___ Check types:

___ filmloops   ___ records
___ filmstrips   ___ tapes
___ other (specify) _____

11. Please make any comments you wish.

Student questionnaire
On use of the library and library tools

Name: _____ | Sex: M F | 1st semester: yes no

A. HOW WOULD YOU GRADE THE LIBRARY SERVICES/FACILITIES YOU HAVE USED?
Do so by marking (+) good, (OK) satisfactory, (-) poor, ( ) have not used:

( ) place to study ( ) journals ( ) reference books
( ) reserve reading ( ) interlibrary loan ( ) reference questions
( ) general reading ( ) microforms ( ) browsing
( ) borrow books ( ) maps ( ) card catalog
( ) xerox service ( ) indexes, abstracts ( ) research

B. YOUR PATTERN OF LIBRARY USE?
Mark with (X):

( ) more than once a week
( ) more than 8 times a semester
( ) a few times
( ) none

C. DID YOU ASK FOR HELP FROM ANY
LIBRARY WORKER? Mark with (X):

( ) yes ( ) no
WERE YOU SATISFIED?
( ) yes ( ) no

Dept. Ed. Serv.

COMPARISON OF HIGH SCHOOL AVERAGES AND PERFORMANCE
BY CLASS AND SEX

Group	Mean H.S. Average			Mean Point Gain			Mean % Improvement			% Passing Eng. Course			% Receiving Credit Following Semester		
	F	M	All	F	M	All	F	M	All	F	M	All	F	M	All
A-Weekly Spring	70.55	73.50	71.68	17.69	22.67	19.05	38	44	39	44	40	43	56	100	71
A-Control	73.72	64.07	71.65	17.07	22.48	18.42	36	48	39	33	25	31	50	75	63
B-Tradi-tional Spring	74.33	69.86	72.93	5.85	9.33	6.59	13	14	13	75	40	67	82	60	75
B-Control	70.96	69.70	70.09	9.46	10.55	10.04	14	18	16	50	36	42	75	56	65
B-Weekly Fall	65.95	76.59	70.33	3.99	4.75	4.24	6	7	7	69	63	67	91	71	83
B-Control	72.36	74.09	73.37	5.61	5.18	5.41	8	10	9	75	57	67	100	86	93
A-Tradi-tional Fall	65.00	73.53	69.59	-3.00	10.00	4.43	-3	15	7	50	43	47	63	71	67
A-Control	70.40	76.74	74.10	8.60	11.74	10.84	12	19	17	38	71	50	43	71	54
AVERAGE	70.41	72.26	71.72	8.15	12.09	9.88	15.5	21.9	18.4	54.3	46.9	51.8	70.0	73.75	71.38

SUMMARY BY TYPE OF INSTRUCTION

	F	M	All	F	M	All	F	M	All	F	M	All	F	M	All
Weekly	68.25	75.05	71.01	10.84	13.71	11.65	22.00	25.50	23.00	56.50	51.50	55.00	73.50	85.50	77.00
Tradi-tional	69.67	71.70	71.26	1.43	9.67	5.51	5.00	14.50	10.00	62.50	41.50	57.00	72.50	65.50	71.00
Control	71.86	71.15	72.30	10.19	12.49	11.18	17.50	23.75	20.25	49.00	47.25	47.50	67.00	72.00	68.75

TWO SEMESTER COMPARISON OF

MEAN GRADE POINT AVERAGES

AND

STUDENT RETENTION

Group	Semester of Experiment		Following Semester		Gain/Loss	
	Student Count	Mean GPA	Student Count	Mean GPA	Student Count	Mean GPA
A--Weekly Spring	14	1.73	11	2.10	-3	+0.37
A--Control	16	1.27	11	0.92	-5	-0.35
B--Traditional Spring	18	1.32	15	1.07	-3	-0.25
B--Control	19	1.22	16	0.91	-3	-0.31
B--Weekly Fall	18	1.53	15	1.85	-3	+0.32
B--Control	15	1.93	14	2.36	-1	+0.43
A--Traditional Fall	15	1.41	10	2.12	-5	+0.71
A--Control	14	1.18	10	1.46	-4	+0.28

SUMMARY COMPARISON BY TYPE OF LIBRARY INSTRUCTION

Weekly	16	1.63	13	1.98	-3	+0.35
Traditional	16.5	1.37	12.5	1.60	-4	+0.23
Control	16	1.40	13	1.41	-3	+0.01

THE MAIN IDEA

I. In paragraphs, newspaper and magazine articles

II. In longer works (e.g., books, plays) and topics

    A. Outlines
       1. description
         a. how to use
         b. how to set up
       2. easy sources
         a. table of contents in factual books
         b. headings in longer articles and books

    B. Digests or synopses
       1. definition and location
       2. examples

I. All reading centers around main ideas. Each paragraph and each article has a main idea, but sometimes it is difficult to find.

A newspaper article, however, makes it easy. In it the main idea is always given in the first sentence or two and is called the LEAD. The LEAD of a news article answers all or most of the 5 W's and H:

WHO -- WHAT -- WHERE -- WHEN -- WHY -- HOW

Once the answer to most of the 5 W's and H is determined in a paragraph or short article, the main idea will have been found.

II. An outline is an organized plan of ideas. It brings together in a logical step by step development, the main ideas of a topic. There are two main uses for outlines: (1) to help you remember things you have read or studied; (2) to help you keep in mind the points you wish to make in a paper or speech.

Usually Roman numerals (I, II, etc.) are used for main topics and capital letters (A, B, etc.) for subtopics. However, jotting down a short, informal outline can help you organize your thoughts to better answer an essay test question.

Often the information for an outline is made easily available within the material being read:

Table of contents: In the front of most factual books there is a table of contents, which lists the chapter titles or main divisions of the book. These chapter headings help you find the main points or ideas of the book. If subtopics are listed under the chapter headings, the table of contents can help you "see" the whole book at a glance.

Headings: Often chapters of books and articles in encyclopedias and magazines are divided into sections by headings. These headings are to call your attention to the main ideas or points of the topic. By putting these headings into an outline you can "see" the whole article at a glance.

III. Digests or synopses are plot summaries for well-known books and plays. If you have trouble understanding the main ideas of a work you are reading and want to review one you read sometime ago, these brief accounts will help you. There are many such sources available. Synopses for individual books and plays can be purchased in bookstores. Collections of synopses are available in the library; the most important ones are located at the reference desk on the first floor. Some of these are:

Haydn, Hiram. Thesaurus of Book Digests, 1956

This has very brief summaries, arranged by title with an author index.

Keller, Helen Rex. Reader's Digest of Books, 1961

This has digests of important works of fiction and non-fiction, arranged by title with an author index.

Magill, Frank. Masterplots, 1968

This is an eight-volume set of plot summaries of novels and plays, and essay reviews of poetry, philosophy, and other works of literature without plots. The index in the last volume should be consulted in order to use the set.

Sprinchorn, Evert. 20th Century Plays in Synopsis, 1965

This has act-by-act summaries of 133 representative dramas by modern playrights, arranged by author with a title index.

NAME: _____

I.   NEWSPAPER

     article: _____

          WHO: _____

          WHAT: _____

          WHEN: _____

          WHERE: _____

          WHY: _____

          HOW: _____

II. ENCYCLOPEDIA

     Look up the topic, _____, in volume __
     of the World Book Encyclopedia. By looking at the headings in the
     article answer the following question and give the number of the
     page on which each answer appears.

     Question: _____

     Answers: 1. _____on page _____

              2. _____on page _____

              3. _____on page _____

              4. _____on page _____

     To check your answer look at the end of the article for an outline
     of the topic. On what page does the outline appear? p. _____

III. DIGESTS and SYNOPSES

     In which digest or synopsis is there a summary of _____

     _____ ?

     _____

     On what pages does the summary appear? _____

Answer the following questions from the Book Review Digest:

Look up the reviews on _____

1. On what page(s) do you find this book reviewed? _____

2. Were the reviews (check one) __favorable, __mixed, __unfavorable?

3. Name two periodicals which carried reviews on this book and which
   can be found in the Brooklyn College library: (1) _____

   _____and (2) _____

PICKING TOPICS

I. Originality

II. Size of assignment

III. Source materials

    A. Availability

B. Types of Defense	Acceptability	Requirement
general knowledge and personal opinion	poor	none
survey	satisfactory	time, access to population
statistical information	good	source citation
expert opinion	good	source citation

IV. Starting point

       The first task in writing a paper is to decide on what topic to write. A well-chosen topic will contribute a lot toward the success of the paper. Here are the main points to consider when choosing a topic:

1. Originality -- Try to pick a topic that is not too popular, i.e., one about which many other students are not likely to have written. Teachers find it difficult to be interested in a paper that is similar to dozens of others they have read. Therefore, avoid topics as abortion and drugs. Pick a topic that is of interest to you.

2. Size of assignment -- Try to match possible topics against the size of the assignment given. The smaller the assignment, the more specific the topic should be. For example, "Abraham Lincoln: The Man and the Politician" would be a good topic for a long research paper, but it is too encompassing a topic for a two for three page paper.

3. Source materials -- Sometimes a topic may be original, interesting and of the right "size" but still not be a good one to pick, because there are not materials (books, magazine

or newspaper articles, etc.) easily available to provide necessary information on it. Just saying "I
think" or "everyone knows" is not good enough.
Teachers want supporting evidence to back up ideas.
Usually this evidence is given in the form of quotes
from experts and/or statistical information, and this
evidence is what the source materials must provide.

4. Starting point -- Therefore, it is often easier, rather than picking
a topic and then searching for evidence to support it,
to start with some interesting material and pick up a
topic from the information in hand.

Name: _____

Name of article: _____

    Author: _____   Page: _____

    Source: _____   Date: _____

Main idea: _____

   Arguments for: 1. _____

               2. _____

               3. _____

Name of article: _____

    Author: _____   Page: _____

    Source: _____   Date: _____

Main idea: _____

   Arguments for: 1. _____

               2. _____

               3. _____

ABOUT THE BOOK

I. Title page

  A. Title and subtitle--what can be determined about the book from its title(s)?

HOW TO TEACH YOUR BABY TO READ

THE
GENTLE
REVOLUTION

by Glenn Doman

Random House | New York

B. <u>Author</u>--what are his qualifications for writing on the subject of the book (this information may be located elsewhere in the book or on the book jacket)?

about the author

GLENN J. DOMAN graduated from the University of Pennsylvania School of Physical Therapy in 1940, and then became a staff member of the Temple University Hospital in Philadelphia. He entered the United States Army as a private in 1941 and retired a lieutenant colonel, having been awarded the D.S.C., the Silver Star, the Bronze Star, the British Military Cross, and other decorations.

In his chosen field he has received the Roberto Simonsen Award from Brazil for his contributions to social science in that nation, the Gold Medal of Honor of Brazil, and others. He is now the Director of The Institutes for the Achievement of Human Potential at Philadelphia.

C. <u>Copyright date</u>--was the book written recently enough to be helpful, e.g., science books must be current (a copyright is granted by the United States government to writers if their works are original and protects their writings from being copied without permission; the date is usually found on the back of the title page)?

First Printing

Library of Congress Catalog Card Number: 64-22442

Manufactured in the United States of America

II. <u>Table</u> <u>of</u> <u>contents</u>--gives, in the form of chapter titles, the
     major divisions or main ideas of the book and tells on
     which page the information begins. Sometimes these
     chapter titles give the support or arguments for the
     author's opinion (proposition) regarding the subject.

table of contents

III. Index--gives an alphabetical listing of the many names, ideas and small topics discussed in the book and tells on which page(s) they are located. These subjects are often called entries, and when there is a division under the subject, they are called sub-entries. If there is another subject closely related to an entry, directions will be given to "see" or "see also" the related subject entry.

From William Glasser, Schools without Failure *(New York: Harper and Row, 1969)*.

232   I N D E X

Colleges, 59, 68, 170–171, 200,
   admittance to, 60–62, 64,
      215–216
Commitment, 22–24, 126–127,
Community, school and, 222-
Conformity, 174–175
Coopersmith, Stanley, 194
   quoted, 195
Counseling and counselors,
      147, 224
   group, 224
Creativity, 206
Culkin, Father John, quoted,
Curriculum, 54–58, 206
   dissatisfaction with, 54

Decision making, 77–79
Delinquents, 1–5, 27, 113
Democracy, 37, 77
Discipline, 23, 87, 89, 124,
      224–226
   at class meetings, 158–159
   school administration and,
   See also Punishment
Discussion, 36–37, 67, 78, 93-
   group, 224–225
   questions for, 163–185
   See also Class meetings

Education (*Continued*)
   value of, 2, 4–5
   vocational, 215
Emotion, 56
   behavior and, 20–21, 42–43
Employment, menial, 9–10
   opportunities for, 5–6
Enrichment program, 212–214

Faculty meetings, 117–121, 157
Failure, in city schools, xiii
   loneliness and, 16–18
   prevention of, by abolishing grading,
      95–108
      by heterogeneous classes, 81–94
      importance of thinking in, 76–81
   problem of, 1–11
   Reality Therapy and, 12–24
   relevance and, 42, 45
   total, 96–97
   types of, 12
Family life, 182–184
   See also Homes; Parents
Family relationships, 2
Fault finding, 129
Friends and friendships, 171–174
Frustration, 40–41
Fullerton, California, 119

IV. BOOK REVIEW DIGEST--gives, from magazines, representative reviews and criticisms for a great number of books. The information includes a brief statement about the purpose (main idea) of each book, tells how "experts" evaluated it and in which issues of magazines the reviews originally appeared.

   To find out if a book has been included in a Book Review Digest volume, look in the volume for the year of the book's copyright date and then under the author's last name. A title and subject index appears at the end of each volume.

   The Book Review Digest can be found in the index area on the first floor of the library.

Name: _____

Answer the following questions from the materials provided:

1. Give the author's name and tell his chief qualification for
   writing this book. _____

2. Give the complete title. _____

3. When was the book copyrighted? _____

   Is it current enough to be of value on the subject? __yes, __no

4. The Table of Contents:

   a. In what chapter does the book give information on the
      problems of nonreaders? _____

   b. State the proposition which the author defends in this book.

      _____

   c. State the arguments with which the author defends his
      proposition.

      1. _____

      2. _____

      3. _____

      4. _____

5. The Index:

   a. Name one main entry that has two or more sub-entries under it.

      _____

   b. What is the "see also" reference under "Homes, broken?"

      _____What additional pages do you find

      listed there? _____

ENCYCLOPEDIAS

For most topics encyclopedias offer the most easily available and convenient source of background information. For this reason they are particularly valuable when a topic is being considered for a paper or a speech. In them both the basic information and range of each topic are given. In addition, encyclopedia articles will often direct readers to related topics and/or books on the topic.

Two general encyclopedias of particular help to students are: World Book Encyclopedia (located near the center of the third floor) and Collier's Encyclopedia (located on the first floor in the open reference section).

World Book Encyclopedia is used like a dictionary (i.e., all the subjects are listed alphabetically; and, for example, information on airplanes would be located in the "A" volume of the set). At the end of many articles related topics are listed and/or titles of books on the subject.

Collier's Encyclopedia like almost all other encyclopedias requires the use of an index. The index is usually in a separate volume at the end of the set, and it often lists related information as sub-entries under the main subject entry. Here is an example of a main entry with some sub-entries and what it means:

NEW YORK UNIVERSITY 17-
    504b; 1-45c; 6-721b;
    12-106d
  Hall of Fame 11-600b
  Journalism 13-643d
--Ill. 17-505d, 485a
--Map 17-496

a	c
b	d

(letters after page
numbers signify on
which quarter of
the page, the in-
formation begins)

The main information on New York University begins on page 504 of volume 17. The University is also referred to on page 45 of volume 1, page 721 of volume 6 and page 106 of volume 12. On page 600 of volume 11 in the article on the Hall of Fame and on page 643 of volume 13 in the article on journalism, the University is mentioned. Pictures of the University will be found on pages 505 and 485 of volume 17. A map of the University will be found on page 496 of volume 17.

There are many other general encyclopedias (i. e., those which cover the whole field of knowledge) in the library; some are available in foreign languages. Other encyclopedias specialize in a particular subject field and, therefore, cover their topics more thoroughly. The Encyclopedia of World Art is an example of a specialized encyclopedia.

Name: _____

Possible topic for use in English 1.2: _____

World Book Encyclopedia:

    1. In what volume is the topic located? ___ On what page(s)? ___

    2. What is the title of the article? _____

    3. Does the article contain any pictures, maps, graphs, etc.?

       ___no ___yes

    4. Does the article refer to:

       a. other articles in the encyclopedia? ___no ___yes

          If yes, name one: _____

       b. books? ___no ___yes If yes, give the title and author

          of one: _____

Collier's Encyclopedia:

    1. On what page in the index volume is the topic listed? _____

       Write down the main entry for the topic as it appears (with

       page number(s), etc.): _____

       _____

       Does the bibliography contain books on the topic? ___no ___yes

    2. In what volume is the topic located? ___ On what pages(s)? ___

    3. Does the article contain any pictures, maps, graphs, etc.?

       ___no ___yes

Preference:

    Which encyclopedia is most helpful for getting information on your

    topic? _____

    Do you still think it is a good topic for your class work?

    ___no ___yes

108 : *Appendix 3*

POINTS TO REMEMBER:

1. Always look in the index volume first (except when using the
   <u>World</u> <u>Book</u> <u>Encyclopedia</u>).

2. Check the copyright date of encyclopedias; they can get "too
   old" just like books. Extremely recent topics will not be
   included in them, but they may appear in the annual (yearly)
   supplements.

3. Although encyclopedias offer excellent background information
   for when a topic is first being studied, instructors prefer
   to have more specific sources (i.e., a book or magazine
   article) cited in research papers.

WORK SHEET FOR USING MAGAZINE (PERIODICAL) ARTICLES IN RESEARCH PAPERS

1. Pick your topic. The choice of topic will largely determine where
the best information can be found, e. g., information on current
issues and problems will largely be found in newspaper and magazine
articles while information on historical topics will largely be
found in books.

2. Go to the READER'S GUIDE or another suitable index (e.g., NEW YORK
TIMES INDEX if you are seeking newspaper articles). Indexes are
generally arranged by years and list all the articles printed in
a large number of periodicals during the year indicated under
subject headings.

3. Look up your topic in the index. Here you may have to be a detective
to find the correct wording for the subject heading needed. For
example, if your topic is on air pollution in New York City, possible headings to look under would be:
                     pollution
                     air pollution
                     New York City
Or if you cannot find the topic word(s) you are seeking, try a syn-
onymous word or phrase, e. g., Afro-Americans--Negroes. Sometimes
the index will help with an instructional "see" note when you have
looked up a term not used in it. "See also" instructions will
direct you to related articles.

4. Copy down the information given for the articles on your topic. Be
sure to copy down all the information needed for a bibliographic note;
in fact, you will save time if you copy the information immediately
into the correct form for the bibliographic entry. 3 x 5 cards are
particularly useful for this purpose.

> *Goldstein, R. "Drugs on the Campus." Saturday Evening Post, 239 (May 21, 1966), pp. 40-4.*

5. Check on the rotary file to see if the Brooklyn College Library carries the magazines, and copy down the call number if it does. The Brooklyn College Library carries most of the magazines listed in READER'S GUIDE, but it does not carry, for example, ladies' magazines like GOOD HOUSEKEEPING and REDBOOK.

6. Locate the magazines on the second floor of the library. If the magazine you are seeking is a year or less old, go to the current periodicals desk. If it is older locate it on the shelves according to its call number just as you would a book. If you have difficulty locating the magazine, ask for help at the current periodicals desk.

7. Take notes from the articles for your paper. Magazines may not be taken out of the library, so either copy notes onto cards (one idea per card), or if the article is particularly helpful xerox the article on the second floor (10 cents per page).

Name: _____

1. General topic for English 1.2: _____

   Specific topic for a single paper: _____

Look specific topic up in a volume of <u>Readers'</u> <u>Guide</u> on the first floor.

Under what heading(s) do articles on the topic appear?

_____

2. Pick out two articles on the topic and prepare one card each for them
   as per the following example:

   DRUGS   ---   DRUG PROBLEMS AND STUDENTS

KENISTON, KENNETH, "STUDENTS,
DRUGS AND PROTEST."
CURRENT, 104 (FEBRUARY,
1969), pp. 5-19.

* AP2
.C9259

3. Do exactly the same thing as in #2 with another volume of the <u>Readers'</u>
   <u>Guide.</u> (When finished there will be four cards in all.)

   Under what heading(s) do articles on the topic appear in this volume?

_____

4. Consult the rotary file to see if the library carries the magazines
   listed on your cards. *Copy down the call numbers for them on the back
   of the cards.

5. Go to the second floor and locate <u>two</u> of the articles on your cards.

6. Take the magazines to the xerox room and have the first page of the
   <u>two</u> articles copied.

Name: _____

Besides magazine articles and books, there are many other sources of information in the library. Two of these sources are the New York Times
and the library's pamphlet file.

Specific topic for a single paper: _____

1a. Look for the topic in the pamphlet file on the first floor next to
the reference desk.

b. Under what heading(s) is there information on the topic? _____

_____   _____

c. How many folders of information are there under the above heading(s)?

_____

2a. Look for the topic in the New York Times Index. (This index is
arranged just like the Reader's Guide and is located near the latter
on the first floor.)

b. Under what heading(s) is there information on the topic? _____

_____   _____

c. Copy down the entry for one article on the topic:

_____

_____

d. Find the above article on microfilm on the second floor and show it to
Miss Martin or Mrs. Breivik.

_____

3. Which source of information was more helpful on this topic?

Check one: _____ New York Times or _____ the pamphlet file.

Before You Write

Most of the work (approximately 2/3) in writing a good and effective term paper takes place before the actual writing begins. Here are those all important pre-writing steps:

I. Pick a topic.
   A. It should be somewhat original and of interest to you.
   B. It should be of a suitable size for the assignment.
   C. There must be resource materials available.
   (Remember: often it helps to look for potential topics in the newspapers and magazines you are reading, so that you will have source materials available from the start.)

II. Main-idea statement. Next to the wise choosing of the topic for a paper, the next most important thing is to clearly and carefully decide on the main idea for the paper. This idea should be a direct statement (never a question).

Here are some questions to ask yourself when writing main-idea statements:
   a. Is it as brief as possible?
   b. Is it as specific as possible?
   c. Does it sound interesting?
   d. Could someone write a paper opposing the point-of-view stated? (Most good main-idea statements are potentially controversial.) If so, would the statement be clearer if the word "should" was used in the statement?

III. Find supportive materials.
   A. Using your main-idea statement as the heading for an outline, write down all the supportive arguments of which you can think; or if you have a magazine or newspaper article that supports your idea, glance through it quickly to see (perhaps the headings will help) what supportive arguments it gives. Test each argument to see if it really supports your main-idea statement by filling in this sentence in your mind:

   I believe...(main-idea statement)...because...(supportive argument)...

   If this sentence sounds feasible, you have found a good supportive argument. Put the supportive arguments in a logical order within the outline.
   B. Consult source materials to find statistical facts, quotes and other information to back up each argument listed in the outline. Write each piece of information on a separate card or piece of paper and put them in the same order as the outline. (To save confusion, number each piece of information the same as the corresponding argument's position in the outline.)
   C. If readings turn up additional arguments to support your idea, add them in your outline at an appropriate place.

Notes

Introduction

1. U.S. Department of Labor. *Occupational Outlook Quarterly* (Washington, D.C.: Government Printing Office, Summer 1974), v.18, p. 5.

2. U.S. Department of Labor. *Occupational Outlook Handbook*. Bulletin 1785 (Washington, D.C.: Government Printing Office, 1974), p. 21.

3. Alan Gartner and Harriet Johnson, "An Examination of College Programs for Paraprofessionals" (mimeographed), (New York: New Careers Development Center, New York University, October 1970), p. [i].

4. University of the State of New York, Bureau of Post-Secondary Continuing Education, *The Demography of the New York Population of Educationally and Economically Disadvantaged Adults* (Albany, N.Y.: State Education Department, 1975), p. 3.

Chapter 1

1. James S. Coleman et al., *Equality of Educational Opportunity* (Washington, D.C.: Government Printing Office, 1966), p. 3.

2. University of the State of New York, Bureau of Post-Secondary Continuing Education, *The Demography of the New York Population of Educationally and Economically Disadvantaged Adults* (Albany, N.Y.: State Education Department, 1975), pp. 19–20.

3. Ibid., p. 15.

4. Thaddeus H. Spratlen, "Financing Inner City Schools: Policy Aspects of Economics, Political and Racial Disparity," *Journal of Negro Education*, 42: 283–307 (Summer 1973).

5. Gene I. Maeroff, "State Issues: School-Aid Revisions Sought," *New York Times*, Oct. 26, 1974, p. 14, col. 5.

6. Joel S. Berke, "Recent Adventures of State School Finance: A Saga of Rocket Ships and Glider Planes," *School Review*, 82: 183–206 (Feb. 1974).

7. Donna E. Shalala and Mary Frase Williams, "State Tax Politics, the Voters, and School Financial Reform," *Phi Delta Kappan*, 56: 10–13 (Sept. 1974).

8. Robert Reinhold, "School Financing Still a Taxing Riddle," *New York Times*, Nov. 16, 1975, education sec., p. 9, col. 1.

9. Iver Peterson, "City U. Cuts $54.6 Million, Modifies Open Admissions," *New York Times*, Dec. 16, 1975, p. 1, col. 1.

10. Merrill Sheils, "Why Johnny Can't Write," *Newsweek*, Dec. 8, 1975, pp. 58–65.

11. K. Patricia Cross, "Learner-centered Curricula," in Dyckman W. Vermilye, ed., *Learner-centered Reform* (San Francisco: Jossey-Bass, 1975), p. 56.

12. Alvin Toffler, *Future Shock* (New York: Bantam Books, 1971), p. 414.

13. Lewis B. Mayhew, "The Future Undergraduate Curriculum," in Alvin C. Eurich, ed., *Campus 1980* (New York: Delacorte, 1968), p. 211.

14. Cross, "Learner-centered Curricula," p. 56.

Chapter 2

1. Douglas M. Knight and Shepley E. Nourse, eds., *Libraries at Large* (New York: Bowker, 1969), p. 482.

2. Albert N. Whiting, "Obligations to the Disadvantaged Student," *Liberal Education*, 55: 229 (May 1969).

3. Knight and Nourse, *Libraries at Large*, p. 482.

4. Education Commission of the States, *The States and Graduate Education* (report no. 59; Denver: Education Commission of the States, Feb. 1975), p. 20.

5. "Open Admissions: American Dream or Disaster?" *Time*, Oct. 19, 1970, p. 63.

6. James A. Colston, "Open Admissions at the City University," speech given at annual spring meeting of Beta Phi Mu International Library Science Honorary Society, Theta Chapter, New York, May 2, 1972, p. 2.

7. City University of New York, *Proceedings of the City University of New York Conference on Open Admissions* (New York: CUNY, 1971), p. 7.

8. Dennis Menzel, "Theoretical Issues Involved in Educating the Disadvantaged" (1969), p. 3 (available from ERIC, no. ED 039 833).

9. Oscar Handlin, *The New-Comers* (Cambridge, Mass.: Harvard Univ. Pr., 1959), p. 88.

10. "Open Admissions: American Dream or Disaster?" p. 66.

11. Ewald B. Nyquist, "Education's Financial Dilemma: Planning for Change or Reacting to Crisis," speech given at sixth meeting of Education Commission of the States, Los Angeles, May 17, 1972 (available from ERIC, no. ED 064 770).

12. Jack H. Aldridge, "Curriculum for Disadvantaged Students in Higher Education," paper presented at 1969 American Personnel and Guidance Association Convention, Las Vegas, Nev., April 1, 1969, p. 6.

13. Whiting, "Obligations," p. 231.

14. Massachusetts University School of Education, *Survey Report of State-funded College Programs for "Disadvantaged" Students in Massachusetts* (Amherst: Massachusetts University School of Education, 1972) (available from ERIC no. ED 063 836).

15. SEEK (Search for Education, Elevation, and Knowledge) began in the City University of New York in September 1966 as a result of a New York State legislative man-

date. High school graduates of poor educational background are motivated, scholastically prepared, and financially assisted to enter college and to meet the requirements of a CUNY senior college. Students up to 30 years of age are accepted in the SEEK program. Every effort is made to provide an educational environment that comprises maximum success experiences.

16. "Open Admissions: American Dream or Disaster?" p. 65.

17. "The Future of SEEK," *New York Times,* Jan. 5, 1976, editorial sec., p. 28, col. 2.

18. Samuel Weiss, "SEEK Program Striving to Ride Out Its Troubles," *New York Times,* May 4, 1975, education sec., p. 21, col. 2.

19. Solomon Resnik and Barbara Kaplan, "Report Card on Open Admissions: Remedial Work Recommended," *New York Times,* May 9, 1971, magazine sec., p. 37.

20. Ibid., p. 42.

21. William T. Trent, "College Compensatory Programs for Disadvantaged Students" (1970), p. 7 (available from ERIC, no. ED 042 394).

22. Exalton A. Delco, Jr., George T. Matthews, and Robert W. Rogers, "Opportunities and Responsibilities for Developing Human Resources," *Liberal Education,* 55: 238 (May 1969).

23. Resnik and Kaplan, "Report Card on Open Admissions," p. 37.

24. Sharad Karkhanis and Betty-Carol Sellen, eds., *A New College Student: The Challenge to the City University Libraries,* papers presented at meeting of Library Association of the City University of New York Institute, New York, Apr. 10, 1969. (Rockaway Park, N.Y.: Scientific Book Service, 1969), p. 25.

25. Delco, Matthews, and Rogers, "Opportunities and Responsibilities," p. 238.

26. M. Ann Petrie, "Up the Down Campus—Notes from a Teacher on Open Admissions," *New York,* May 17, 1971, p. 30.

27. David E. Lavin and Richard Silberstein, *Student Retention under Open Admissions at the City University of New York: September 1970 Enrollees Followed through Four Semesters* (New York: CUNY Office of Program and Policy Research, 1974), p. 12.

28. Jerry Adler, "Ax Will Leave College in Splinters: Kneller," *New York Times,* Nov. 2, 1975, Living in Brooklyn sec., p. 1.

29. Edward B. Fiske, "Kibbee Proposes 20% Cut in Scope of City University," *New York Times,* Sept. 15, 1975, p. 1+, col. 6.

30. Resnik and Kaplan, "Report Card on Open Admissions," p. 32.

31. Aldridge, "Curriculum for Disadvantaged," p. 41.

32. Patricia B. Knapp, "The Academic Library Response to New Directions in Undergraduate Education" (Minneapolis: Univ. of Minnesota Library School, 1970), p. 17 (available from ERIC, no. ED 039 390).

33. Ibid., p. 5.

Chapter 3

1. Douglas Waples, *The Library: The Evaluation of Higher Institutions* (Chicago: Univ. of Chicago Pr., 1936), 4: 77.

2. Patricia B. Knapp, "The Academic Library Response to New Directions in Undergraduate Education (Minneapolis: Univ. of Minnesota Library School, 1970), p. 17 (available from ERIC, no. ED 039 390).

3. Patricia B. Knapp, "The Montieth Library Project," *College and Research Libraries,* 22: 257 (July 1961).

4. F. W. Lancaster, "User Education: The Next Major Thrust in Information Science?" *Journal of Education for Librarianship,* 11: 56 (Summer 1970).

5. Evelyn Steel Little, *Instruction in the Use of Books and Libraries in Colleges and Universities* (Ann Arbor: Univ. of Michigan Library, 1936).

6. A. C. Eurich, "The Significance of Library Reading among College Students," *School and Society,* 36: 96 (July 16, 1932).

7. Lloyd A. Kramer and Martha B. Kramer, "The College Library and the Drop-Out," *College and Research Libraries,* 31: 310 (July 1968).

8. Patrick Barkey, "Patterns of Student Use of a College Library," *College and Research Libraries,* 26: 115 (Mar. 1965).

9. R. Vernon Ritter, "An Investigation of Classroom-Library Relationships on a College Campus as Seen in Recorded Circulation and GPA's," *College and Research Libraries,* 29: 30 (Jan. 1968).

10. Robert P. Haro, "Academic Library Service Breakthrough to Penetrate Learning Barriers," in Patricia Schuman and Betty-Carol Sellen, eds., *Libraries for the 70's* (New York: Queens College, 1970), p. 19.

11. Millicent C. Palmer, "Why Academic Library Instruction?" in Sul H. Lee, ed., *Library Orientation* (Ann Arbor, Mich.: Pierian Pr., 1972), p. 3.

12. Trevor Dupuy, *Ferment in College Libraries* (Washington, D.C.: Communication Service, 1968), pp. 28–29.

13. Statement of admissions policy, adopted by New York City Board of Higher Education, Nov. 12, 1969.

14. "Open Admissions: Unfair Competition?" *Change* (Sept./Oct. 1970), p. 17.

15. Brooklyn College Library, "Report of the Open Admissions Committee" (unpublished report, Brooklyn College, Mar. 9, 1970), pp. 2–3, 8.

16. Ibid., p. 7.

17. Dorothy M. Knoell, "The Special Needs of New Students for Service Relating to the Library Function," in Sharad Karkhanis and Betty-Carol Sellen, eds., *A New College Student: The Challenge to City University Libraries* (Rockaway Park, N.Y.: Scientific Book Service, 1969), p. 41.

18. This investigation was conducted in connection with a seminar at Columbia School of Library Service under the supervision of Maurice F. Tauber. Richard H. Logsdon, CUNY dean for libraries, gave it his support, and librarians at Brooklyn, City, and Hunter colleges were consulted during the preparation of the questionnaire (*see* appendix A).

19. Library Association of the City University of New York Executive Council, "Resolution on Open Admissions," *LACUNY Journal,* 1: 36 (Winter 1972).

20. Thomas W. Shaughnessy, "Library Services to Educationally Disadvantaged Students," *College and Research Libraries,* 36: 443–48 (Nov. 1975).

Chapter 4

1. Herbert Ravetch, *Individualization of Instruction: The Junior College Takes a Page from the Elementary-Secondary Notebook* (Los Angeles: Univ. of California, 1968), p. 18 (available from ERIC, no. ED 031 211).

2. "Conference on Library Services for the Disadvantaged: Proceedings Summary," Harriman, N.Y., Dec. 10–11, 1964, p. 4 (available from ERIC, no. ED 022 509).

3. Exalton A. Delco, Jr., George T. Matthews, and Robert W. Rogers, "Opportunities and Responsibilities for Developing Human Resources," *Liberal Education,* 55: 235–43 (May 1969).

4. Patricia B. Knapp, "The Montieth Library Project," *College and Research Libraries,* 22: 257 (July 1961).

5. Dan Lacey and Virginia H. Matthews, "Social Change and the Library" (Washington, D.C.: National Advisory Commission on Libraries and the National Book Committee, Dec. 1967), p. 22 (available from ERIC, no. ED 022 483).

6. Harvie Branscomb, *Teaching with Books* (Chicago: Association of American Colleges, 1940), pp. vii–x.

7. Louis Shores, "The Library Arts College, a Possibility in 1954?" *School and Society,* 41: 110–14 (Jan. 26, 1935).

8. Louis R. Wilson, "The Use of the Library in Instruction," in *1941 Proceedings of the Institute for Administrative Officers of Higher Institutions* (Chicago: Univ. of Chicago Pr., 1941), pp. 115–27.

9. Louis Shores, "The Library-University," *School and Society,* 99: 163–66 (Mar. 1971).

10. Douglas M. Knight and Nourse E. Shepley, eds., *Libraries at Large* (New York: Bowker, 1969), pp. 103–5.

Chapter 5

1. Iver Peterson, "City U. Cuts $54.6 Million, Modifies Open Admissions," *New York Times,* Dec. 16, 1975, pp. 1+.

2. University of the State of New York, Bureau of Post-Secondary Education, *The Demography of the New York Population of Educationally and Economically Disadvantaged Adults* (Albany, N.Y.: State Education Department, 1975), p. 1.

3. U.S. Department of Health, Education and Welfare, Social and Rehabilitation Service, *Overview Study of Employment of Paraprofessionals,* research report no. 3, National Study of Social Welfare and Rehabilitation Workers, Work and Organizational Contexts (Washington, D.C.: Government Printing Office, 1974), p. 40.

4. James S. Coleman, et al., *Equality of Educational Opportunity* (Washington, D.C.: Government Printing Office, 1966), p. 21.

5. Peterson, "City U. Cuts $54.6 Million, Modifies Open Admissions," p. 1.

6. Eleanor Hall, *Attitudes of City University of New York Students toward Open Admissions* (Washington, D.C.: University Corp., 1971) (available from ERIC, no. ED 055 556).

7. Ezra A. Naughton, "What You See Is What You Get: Black Student/White Campus," in Dyckman W. Vermilye, ed., *The Expanded Campus* (San Francisco: Jossey-Bass, 1972), pp. 57–58.

8. Coleman et al., *Equality of Educational Opportunity,* p. 22.

9. City University of New York, *Proceedings of the City University of New York Conference on Open Admissions* (New York, 1971), p. 7.

10. Angelo Dispenzieri et al., "College Performance of Disadvantaged Students as a Function of Ability and Personality," *Journal of Counseling Psychology,* 18: 298–305 (July 1971).

11. Samuel M. Burt and Herbert E. Striver, *Toward Greater Industry and Government Involvement in Manpower Development* (Kalamazoo, Mich.: W. E. Upjohn Institute for Employment Research, 1968), p. 4.

12. CUNY, *Proceedings*, p. 28.

13. "Harlem to Harvard—and Back," *Time*, Oct. 19, 1970, p. 64.

14. Naughton, "What You See," p. 60.

15. Frank Riessman, "Strategies and Suggestions for Training Nonprofessionals," in Bernard G. Guerney, Jr., ed., *Psycho-Therapeutic Agents* (New York: Holt, Rinehart and Winston, 1969), p. 163.

16. Naughton, "What You See," p. 62.

17. Robert L. Williams, "What Are We Learning from Current Programs for Disadvantaged Students?" *Journal of Higher Education*, 40: 279 (Apr. 1969).

18. Theodore J. Marchese, "Toward a More Effective Experience for Freshmen," paper presented at CASC Workshop, Spring Arbor, Mich., Aug. 10, 1972 (available from ERIC, no. ED 065 106).

19. Burt and Striver, *Toward Greater Industry and Government Involvement*, p. 4.

20. J. Douglas Brown, *The Liberal University: An Institutional Analysis* (New York: McGraw-Hill, 1969), p. 83.

21. Exalton A. Delco, Jr., George T. Matthews, and Robert W. Rogers, "Opportunities and Responsibilities for Developing Human Resources," *Liberal Education*, 55: 238 (May 1969).

22. Frances Cerra, "If a School Flunks Must Student Pay?" *New York Times*, May 4, 1975, sec. 13, p. 1.

Chapter 6

1. William Vernon Jackson, "The Interpretation of Public Services," *Library Trends*, 3: 189 (Oct. 1954).

2. Arthur P. Young, Morell Boone, and Carol Salverson, "Survey of User Education in New York State Libraries," paper presented at New York Library Association Annual Conference, New York, Oct. 6, 1971, p. 4 (available from ERIC, no. ED 055 621).

3. Frederic R. Hartz, "Freshmen Library Orientation: A Need for a New Approach," *College and Research Libraries*, 26: 228 (May 1965).

4. Richard Trent, "The Student: Programs and Problems," in Sharad Karkhanis and Betty-Carol Sellen, eds., *A New College Student: The Challenge to City University Libraries* (Rockaway Park, N.Y.: Scientific Book Service, 1969), p. 19.

5. Frances Henne, "Instruction in the Use of Libraries and Library Use by Students," in Maurice F. Tauber and Irlene R. Stephens, eds., *Conference on the Use of Printed and Audio-Visual Materials for Instructional Purposes* (New York: Columbia Univ. Pr., 1966), pp. 164–90.

6. John Lubans, Jr., *Educating the Library User* (New York: Bowker, 1974).

7. James Kennedy, "Question: A Separate Course in Bibliography or Course Related Library Instruction?" in Sul H. Lee, ed., *Library Orientation* (Ann Arbor, Mich.: Pierian Pr., 1972), p. 25.

8. Thomas V. Atkins, "Libraries and Open Admissions," *LACUNY Journal*, 1: 6 (Winter 1972).

9. Catherine Brody, "Profile of a Librarian: Dorothy Simon," *LACUNY Journal*, 1: 8–11 (Winter 1972).

10. Patricia B. Knapp, *The Montieth College Library Experiment* (New York: Scarecrow, 1966), p. 112.

11. Ibid., p. 51.

12. Swarthmore College, *Critique of a College* (Swarthmore, Pa.: Swarthmore College, 1967), p. 350.

13. "The Council on Library Resources," *Library of Congress Information Bulletin,* Nov. 18, 1971, p. 653.

14. Howard W. Dillon, "The Teaching Library at Sangamon State University," *Journal of Academic Librarianship,* 1:4–7 (Sept. 1975).

15. J. R. Kennedy, "Integrated Library Instruction," *Library Journal,* 95:1453 (Apr. 15, 1970).

16. Maria Wojcik, "Academic Library Instruction," *College and Research Libraries,* 26: 399 (Sept. 1965).

17. Douglas M. Knight and Nourse E. Shepley, eds., *Libraries at Large* (New York: Bowker, 1969), p. 115.

18. Sharad Karkhanis and Betty-Carol Sellen, eds., *A New College Student: The Challenge to City University Libraries,* papers presented at Library Association of CUNY Institute, New York, Apr. 10, 1969 (Rockaway Park, N.Y.: Scientific Book Service, 1969), p. 4.

19. Patricia B. Knapp, "The Academic Library Response to New Directions in Undergraduate Education" (Minneapolis: Univ. of Minnesota Library School, 1970), p. 5 (available from ERIC, no. ED 039 390).

20. Robert P. Haro, "Academic Library Service Breakthrough to Penetrate Learning Barriers," in Patricia Schuman and Betty-Carol Sellen, eds., *Libraries for the 70's* (New York: Queens College, 1970), p. 15.

21. John Lubans, Jr., "Study of the Library Use Habits and Attitudes of 'Academic Opportunity Students,'" unpublished study, Univ. of Colorado Libraries, 1970.

22. Norah E. Jones, "The UCLA Experience: An Undergraduate Library for Undergraduates," *Wilson Library Bulletin,* 45 (Feb. 1971).

23. Miriam Dudley, "Instruction in Library Skills at UCLA," in *Instruction in the Use of the College and University Library: Selected Conference Papers* (July 13–14, 1970) (Berkeley: Univ. of California School of Library Service, 1970), pp. 1–10 (available from ERIC, no. ED 045 103).

24. The most recent is Miriam Dudley, *Workbook in Library Skills: A Self-directed Course in the Use of UCLA's College Library* (Los Angeles: Univ. of California Library, 1973).

25. Walter Wagner, "On Integrating Libraries and Classrooms," *Learning Today,* 6: 48–62 (Winter 1973).

26. Mordine Mallory, "The New College Student and the Library," in Karkhanis and Sellen, eds., *A New College Student,* pp. 32–40.

27. Sylvia Hart Wright, "A Pre-College for the Disadvantaged," *Library Journal,* 95: 2884–87 (Sept. 15, 1970).

28. Knapp, "The Academic Library Response," p. 17.

Chapter 7

1. This experiment was part of the work toward my D.L.S. degree at Columbia University School of Library Service, with Dr. Oliver B. Lilley as advisor.

2. City College, *The Faculty Senate News,* Sept. 1970, p. 6.

3. Lillian Zach, "The IQ Debate," *Today's Education,* 61: 40–43 (Sept. 1972).

4. Education Testing Service, *Guide to the Use of GRE Scores in Graduate Admissions, 1971–2* (Princeton, N.J.: Educational Testing Service, 1971), p. 15.

5. William T. Trent, "College Compensatory Programs for Disadvantaged Students" (1970) p. 1 (available from ERIC, no. ED 042 394).

6. James A. Colston, "Open Admissions at the City University," speech given at annual spring meeting of Beta Phi Mu International Library Science Honorary Society, Theta Chapter, New York, May 2, 1972.

7. Letter from Justin L. Dunn, assistant dean and director of admissions, Brooklyn College, Oct. 29, 1973.

8. Patricia B. Knapp, *The Montieth College Library Experience* (New York: Scarecrow, 1966), p. 71.

9. City University of New York, *Proceedings of the City University of New York Conference on Open Admissions* (New York, 1971), p. 83.

10. Knapp, *Montieth College Library Experience,* p. 62.

11. Ibid., p. 111.

12. John Lubans, Jr., "Study of the Library Use Habits and Attitudes of 'Academic Opportunity Students,' " unpublished study, Univ. of Colorado Libraries, 1970.

13. Richard Trent, "The Student: Programs and Problems," in Sharad Karkhanis and Betty-Carol Sellen, eds., *A New College Student: The Challenge to City University Libraries* (Rockaway Park, N.Y.: Scientific Book Service, 1969), p. 19.

14. Albert N. Whiting, "Obligations to the Disadvantaged Student," *Liberal Education,* 55: 233 (May 1969).

15. CUNY, *Proceedings,* p. 30.

16. Mordine Mallory, "The New College Student and the Library," in Karkhanis and Sellen, eds., *A New College Student,* p. 39.

17. Jack H. Aldridge, "Curriculum for Disadvantaged Students in Higher Education," paper presented at 1969 American Personnel and Guidance Association Convention, Las Vegas, Nevada, Apr. 1, 1969, p. 1.

Chapter 8

1. Letter from Charles D. Wantman, registrar, Brooklyn College, Sept. 13, 1973.

2. Assignment based on pages from Glenn J. Doman, *How to Teach Your Baby to Read: The Gentle Revolution* (New York: Random House, 1964).

3. Mordine Mallory, "The New College Student and the Library," in Sharad Karkhanis and Betty-Carol Sellen, eds., *A New College Student: The Challenge to City University Libraries* (Rockaway Park, N.Y.: Scientific Book Service, 1969), p. 39.

4. Norah E. Jones, "The UCLA Experience: An Undergraduate Library for Undergraduates," *Wilson Library Bulletin,* 45: 588 (Feb. 1971).

5. City University of New York, *Proceedings of the City University of New York Conference on Open Admissions* (New York, 1971), p. 28.

Chapter 9

1. Patricia B. Knapp, *The Montieth College Experiment* (New York: Scarecrow, 1966), p. 51.

2. Sylvia Hart Wright, "Backing Up a Remedial, Pre-College Program," unpublished paper, City College of New York, 1965, p. 13.

3. Thomas W. Shaughnessy, "Library Services to Educationally Disadvantaged Students," *College and Research Libraries,* 36: 445–46 (Nov. 1975).

4. Catherine Brody, "Profiles of a Librarian: Dorothy Simon," *LACUNY Journal*, 1: 8–9 (Winter 1972).

5. D. H. Revill, "Teaching Methods in the Library: A Survey from the Educational Point of View," *Library World*, 71: 243–49 (Feb. 1970).

6. Patricia B. Knapp, *The Academic Response to New Directions in Undergraduate Education* (Minneapolis: Univ. of Minnesota Library School, 1970), p. 4 (available from ERIC, no. ED 039 390).

Chapter 10

1. Francis Cerra, "If a School Flunks, Must Student Pay?" *New York Times*, May 4, 1975, education sec., p. 14.

2. Patricia K. Cross, "Learner-centered Curricula" in Dyckman W. Vermilye, ed., *Learner-centered Reform* (San Francisco: Jossey-Bass, 1975), p. 59.

3. Howard R. Bowen, "Teaching and Learning in 2000 A.D.," in *Learner-centered Reform*, p. 160.

4. Paul C. Reinert, "Pluralism and Diversity in Higher Education," in *Learner-centered Reform*, pp. 35–38.

5. John G. Williamson, "Swarthmore College's 'Teaching Library' Proposals," *Drexel Library Quarterly*, 7: 211 (July and Oct. 1971).

6. Mary Watson Hymon, "Libraries, Librarians in a College Reading Program," paper presented at Seminar for Directors of College and University Reading Centers, International Reading Association Convention, Anaheim, Calif., May 6–19, 1970 (available from ERIC, no. ED 045 292).

7. Ibid., p. 1.

8. Zita Cantwell, "Responses of Graduating Seniors—Open Admissions and Educational Opportunities Program Students—to a Survey Questionnaire on Brooklyn College Open Admissions Services," Brooklyn College Office of Testing and Research (May 1974).

9. Stephanie Koren, "Some Thoughts on Bibliographic Instruction," *New York Library Association Bulletin*, 23: 11 (Oct. 1975).

10. Howard E. Gruber and Morris S. Weitman, "Cognitive Processes in Higher Education: Curiosity and Critical Thinking," paper presented at Western Psychological Association Meeting, San Jose, Calif., Apr. 1960.

11. Arthur P. Young, Morell Boone, and Carol Salverson, "Survey on User Education in New York State Academic Libraries," paper presented at New York Library Association Annual Conference, New York, Oct. 6, 1971, p. 3 (available from ERIC, no. ED 055 621).

12. Verna V. Melum, "1971 Survey of Library Orientation and Instruction Programs," *Drexel Library Quarterly*, 7: 225–53 (July and Oct. 1971).

13. Bernard G. Guerney, Jr., *Psycho-Therapeutic Agents* (New York: Holt, Rinehart and Winston, 1969), pp. 246–48.

14. Massachusetts University School of Education, *Survey Report of State-funded College Programs for "Disadvantaged" Students in Massachusetts* (Amherst: Massachusetts Univ., 1972), p. 17 (available from ERIC, no. ED 063 836).

15. Richard M. Bossone, "The Writing Problems of Remedial English Students in Community Colleges of the City of New York" (1969) (available from ERIC, no. ED 028 778).

124 : *Notes*

16. Dennis Menzel, "Theoretical Issues Involved in Educating the Disadvantaged" (1969), pp. 1, 4 (available from ERIC, no. ED 039 833).
17. Exalton A. Delco, Jr., George T. Matthews, and Robert W. Rogers, "Opportunities and Responsibilities for Developing Human Resources," *Liberal Education* 55: 239 (May 1969).
18. J. Periam Danton, *Book Selection and Collections: A Comparison of German and American University Libraries* (New York: Columbia Univ. Pr., 1963), pp. 56–57.
19. Menzel, "Theoretical Issues," p. 5.
20. John Frantz, "The New College Student and the Library," in Sharad Karkhanis and Betty-Carol Sellen, eds., *A New College Student: The Challenge to City University Libraries* (Rockaway Park, N.Y.: Scientific Book Service, 1969), pp. 31–32.

Sources Consulted

Monographs

Brown, J. Douglas. *The Liberal University: An Institutional Analysis.* New York: McGraw-Hill, 1969.

Burt, Samuel M., and Striver, Herbert E. *Toward Greater Industry and Government Involvement in Manpower Development.* Kalamazoo, Mich.: W. E. Upjohn Institute for Employment Research, Sept. 1968.

City University of New York. Office of Program and Policy Research. *Review of the Evaluative Literature on Open Admissions at CUNY.* New York: City Univ. of New York, Oct. 1974.

Coleman, James S.; Campbell, Ernest Q.; Hobson, Carol J.; McPartland, James; Mood, Alexander M.; Weinfeld, Frederic D.; and York, Robert L. *Equality of Educational Opportunity.* Washington, D.C.: Government Printing Office, 1966.

Council for Basic Education. *Open Admissions: The Pros and Cons.* Washington, D.C.: Council for Basic Education, 1972.

Dudley, Miriam. *Workbook in Library Skills: A Self-directed Course in the Use of UCLA's College Library.* Los Angeles: Univ. of California Library, 1973.

Eurich, Alvin C. *Campus 1980.* New York: Delacorte, 1968.

Gartner, Alan, and Johnson, Harriet. "An Examination of College Programs for Paraprofessionals" (mimeographed). New York: New York Univ., New Careers Development Center, Oct. 1970.

Handlin, Oscar. *The Newcomers.* Cambridge, Mass.: Harvard Univ. Pr., 1959.

Henne, Francis. "Instruction in the Use of Library and Library Use by Students." *Conference on the Use of Printed and Audio-Visual Materials for Instructional*

125

Purposes. Eds. Maurice F. Tauber and Irlene Roemer Stephens. New York: Columbia Univ. Pr., 1966.

Karkhanis, Sharad. *Open Admissions: A Bibliography, 1968–1973.* New York: City Univ. of New York, Office of the Chancellor, 1974.

Knapp, Patricia B. *The Montieth College Library Experiment.* New York: Scarecrow, 1966.

Knight, Douglas M., and Nourse, E. Shepley, eds. *Libraries at Large.* New York: Bowker, 1969.

Lavin, David E., and Silberstein, Richard. *Student Retention under Open Admissions at the City University of New York: September 1970 Enrollees Followed through Four Semesters.* New York: City Univ. of New York, Office of Program and Policy Research, 1974.

Little, Evelyn Steel. *Instruction in the Use of Books and Libraries in Colleges and Universities.* Ann Arbor: Univ. of Michigan Library, 1936.

Lubans, Jr., John. *Educating the Library User.* New York: Bowker, 1974.

Mews, Hazel. *Reader Instruction in Colleges and Universities.* Hamden, Conn.: Linnet Books, 1972.

National Education Association. Education Policies Commission. *Manpower and Education.* Washington, D.C.: National Education Association, 1956.

Piesco, Judith; Shrier, Irene; and Podell, Lawrence. *Review of the Evaluative Literature on Open Admissions at CUNY.* New York: City Univ. of New York, Office of Program and Policy Research, Oct. 1974.

Shrier, Irene, and Lavin, David E. *Open Admissions: A Bibliography for Research and Application.* New York: City Univ. of New York, Office of Program and Policy Research, 1974.

Stone, C. Walter, comp. *Academic Change and the Library Function.* Pittsburgh: Pennsylvania Library Association, 1970.

Swarthmore College. *Critique of a College.* Swarthmore, Pa.: Swarthmore College, 1967.

Trinknew, Charles L., ed. *Teaching for Better Use of Libraries.* Hamden, Conn.: Shoe String Pr., 1970.

U.S. Department of Health, Education and Welfare. Social and Rehabilitation Service. *Overview Study of Employment of Paraprofessionals* (research report no. 3, National Study of Social Welfare and Rehabilitation Workers, Work, and Organizational Contexts). Washington, D.C.: Government Printing Office, 1974.

U.S. President's Science Advisory Committee. *Science, Government, and Information.* Washington, D.C.: Government Printing Office, 1963.

University of the State of New York. Bureau of Post-Secondary Continuing Education. *The Demography of the New York Population of Educationally and Economically Disadvantaged Adults.* Albany, N.Y.: State Education Department, 1975.

Vermilye, Dyckman W., ed. *The Expanded Campus* (Current Issues in Higher Education, 1975). San Francisco: Jossey-Bass, 1975.

————, ed. *Learner-centered Reform* (Current Issues in Higher Education, 1972). San Francisco, Jossey-Bass, 1972.

Periodical Articles

Atkins, Thomas V. "Libraries and Open Admissions." *LACUNY Journal,* 1(Winter 1972), 3–7.

Barkey, Patrick. "Patterns of Student Use of a College Library." *College and Research Libraries,* 26(Mar. 1965), 115–18.

Bechtel, Joan M. "A Possible Contribution of the Library-College Idea to Modern Education." *Drexey Library Quarterly,* 7(July and Oct. 1971), 189–201.

Brody, Catherine. "Profile of a Librarian: Dorothy Simon." *LACUNY Journal,* 1(Winter 1972), 8–11.

Clapp, Verner W. "Three Ages of Reference Work." *Special Libraries,* 57(July–Aug. 1966), 379–84.

Colberg, Donald A. "Schools and Libraries Need Survival Kits." *Library-College Journal,* 4(Winter 1971), 27–33.

Delco, Exalton A., Jr.; Matthews, George T.; and Rogers, Robert W. "Opportunities and Responsibilities for Developing Human Resources." *Liberal Education,* 55(May 1969), 235–43.

Dillon, Howard W. "The Teaching Library at Sangamon State University." *Journal of Academic Librarianship,* 1(Sept. 1975), 4–7.

Eurich, A. C. "The Significance of Library Reading among College Students." *School and Society,* 36(July 16, 1932), 92–96.

"Harlem to Harvard—and Back." *Time,* Oct. 19, 1970, p. 64.

Haro, Robert P. "Floating Academic Librarian." *American Libraries,* 2(Dec. 1971), 1169–73.

Hartz, Frederic R. "Freshman Library Orientation: A Need for a New Approach." *College and Research Libraries,* 26(May 1965), 227–231.

Haywood, C. Robert. "Independent Study for Freshmen." *Improving College and University Teaching,* 16(Autumn 1968), 279–80.

Hechinger, Fred M. "What Open Admission Does and Does Not Mean." *New York Times,* Oct. 11, 1970, magazine sec., p. 9.

Henning, Patricia A. "Research on Integrated Library Instruction." *Drexel Library Quarterly,* 7(July and Oct. 1971), 339–41.

Jackson, William Vernon. "The Interpretation of Public Services." *Library Trends,* 3(Oct. 1954), 188–201.

Jones, Norah E. "The UCLA Experience: An Undergraduate Library for Undergraduates." *Wilson Library Bulletin,* 45(Feb. 1971), 584–90.

Kennedy, J. R. "Integrated Library Instruction." *Library Journal,* 95(Apr. 15, 1970), 1450–53.

Knapp, Patricia B. "The Montieth Library Project." *College and Research Libraries,* 22(July 1961), 256–63+.

Kramer, Lloyd A., and Kramer, Martha B. "The College Library and the Drop-Out." *College and Research Libraries,* 31(July 1968), 310–12.

128 : *Sources Consulted*

Lancaster, F. W. "User Education: The Next Major Thrust in Information Science?" *Journal of Education for Librarianship*, 11(Summer 1970), 55–63.

Lane, David O. "The City University of New York and Open Enrollment." *New York State Library*, 31(Jan./Feb. 1972), 73–75.

Melum, Verna V. "1971 Survey of Library Orientation and Instruction Programs." *Drexel Library Quarterly*, 7(July and Oct. 1971), 225–53.

"Open Admissions: Unfair Competition?" *Change* (Sept./Oct. 1970), p. 17.

Palmer, Millicent C. "Library Instruction at Southern Illinois University, Edwardsville." *Drexel Library Quarterly*, 7(July and Oct. 1971), 255–76.

Perry, Margaret. "Race and Education." *American Libraries*, 2(Nov. 1971), 1051–54.

Petrie, M. Ann. "Up the Down Campus—Notes from a Teacher on Open Admissions." *New York*, May 17, 1971, pp. 36–40.

Phipps, Barbara. "Library Instruction for the Undergraduate." *College and Research Libraries*, 29(Sept. 1968), 411–23.

Pifer, Alan. "Toward a Coherent Set of National Policies for Higher Education." *Liberal Education*, 54(Mar. 1968), 5–19.

Reinhold, Robert. "School Financing Still a Taxing Riddle." *New York Times*, Nov. 16, 1975, education sec., p. 9.

Resnick, Solomon, and Kaplan, Barbara. "Report Card on Open Admissions: Remedial Work Recommended." *New York Times*, May 9, 1971, magazine sec., pp. 26–46.

Revill, D. H. "Teaching Methods in the Library: A Survey from the Educational Point of View." *Library World*, 71(Feb. 1970), 243–49.

Ritter, R. Vernon. "An Investigation of Classroom-Library Relationships on a College Campus as Seen in Recorded Circulation and GPA's." *College and Research Libraries*, 29(Jan. 1968), 30–40.

Shaughnessy, Thomas W. "Library Services to Educationally Disadvantaged Students." *College and Research Libraries*, 36(Nov. 1975), 443–48.

Sheils, Merrill. "Why Johnny Can't Write." *Newsweek*, Dec. 8, 1975, pp. 58–65.

Vogel, J. Thomas. "A Critical Overview of the Evaluation of Library Instruction." *Drexel Library Quarterly*, 8(July 1972), 315–23.

Wagner, Walter. "On Integrating Libraries and Classrooms." *Learning Today*, 6(Winter 1973), 48–62.

Wasserman, Paul, and Daniel, Evelyn. "The Birth of LIST." *Library Journal*, 95(Nov. 15, 1970), 3879–83.

White, Carl M. "Services to Scholars." *Library Trends*, 3(Oct. 1954), 148–63.

Whiting, Albert N. "Obligations to the Disadvantaged Student." *Liberal Education*, 55(May 1969), 229–34.

Williams, Robert L. "What Are We Learning from Current Programs for Disadvantaged Students?" *Journal of Higher Education*, 40(Apr. 1969), 274–85.

Williamson, John G. "Swarthmore College's 'Teaching Library' Proposals." *Drexel Library Quarterly*, 7(July and Oct. 1971), 203–15.

Wojcik, Maria. "Academic Library Instruction." *College and Research Libraries*, 21(Sept. 1965), 399–400.

Wright, Sylvia Hart. "A Pre-College Program for the Disadvantaged." *Library Journal,* 95(Sept. 15, 1970), 2884–87.

ERIC

Aldridge, Jack H. "Curriculum for Disadvantaged Students in Higher Education." Paper presented at 1969 American Personnel and Guidance Association Convention, Las Vegas, Nev., Apr. 1, 1969. Available from ERIC, no. ED 031 156.

American Council on Education. "Characteristics of Freshmen Students at the City University of New York, 1972." Available from ERIC, no. ED 055 542.

Bracey, Randolph, Jr. "Compensatory Educational Program—Is There a Place in Higher Education?" Paper submitted to First National Congress of Black Professionals in Higher Education, Austin, Texas, Apr. 5–7, 1972. Available from ERIC, no. ED 062 451.

Brody, Laurence. "Advantages for the Disadvantaged: New Programs." Paper presented at convention of American College Personnel Association and American Personnel and Guidance Association, Las Vegas, Nev., Mar. 1969. Available from ERIC, no. ED 033 993.

"Conference on Library Services for the Disadvantaged: Proceedings Summary." Harriman, N.Y., Dec. 10–11, 1964. Available from ERIC, no. ED 022 509.

Dudley, Miriam. "Instruction in Library Skills at UCLA." *Instruction in the Use of the College and University Library: Selected Conference Papers* (July 13–14, 1970). Berkeley: Univ. of California School of Library Service, 1970, pp. 1–10. Available from ERIC, no. ED 045 103.

Haak, John R. "Goal Determination and the Undergraduate Library." Paper presented at Institute on Training for Service in Undergraduate Libraries, San Diego, California Univ., Aug. 17–21, 1970. Available from ERIC, no. ED 042 474.

Hall, Eleanor. *Attitudes of City University of New York Students toward Open Admissions.* Washington, D.C.: University Corp., 1971. Available from ERIC, no. ED 055 556.

Hood, Wenford L. "Higher Education for the Disadvantaged in New York State: A Summary Report of Programs of Higher Education for the Disadvantaged at Colleges and Universities in New York State." Plattsburgh, N.Y.: State Univ. at Plattsburgh, Jan. 1969. Available from ERIC, no. ED 031 993.

Hyman, Seymour C. "The City University of New York's Open Admissions Program: A Reply to an Article by Rowland Evans and Robert Novak." New York: City Univ. of New York, Jan. 4, 1971. Available from ERIC, no. ED 051 732.

Hymon, Mary Watson. "Libraries, Librarians in a College Reading Program." Paper presented at seminar for directors of college and university reading centers, International Reading Association Convention, Anaheim, Calif., May 6–19, 1970. Available from ERIC, no. ED 045 292.

Jordon, Robert; Goudeau, John M.; and Shores, Louis. *Impact of the Academic Library on the Educational Program.* Durham, N.C.: Duke Univ., 1967. Available from ERIC, no. ED 013 351.

Knapp, Patricia B. "The Academic Library Response to New Directions in Under-graduate Education." Minneapolis: Univ. of Minnesota Library School, 1970. Available from ERIC, no. ED 039 390.

———. "The Library, the Undergraduate and the Teaching Faculty." Paper presented at Institute on Training for Service in Undergraduate Libraries, San Diego, California Univ., Aug. 17–21, 1970. Available from ERIC, no. ED 042 475.

Knoell, Dorothy M. "The 'New Student' in the Community Colleges." Paper presented at Annual Meeting of American Educational Research Association, Chicago, Apr. 6, 1972. Available from ERIC, no. ED 061 156.

Lee, Sul H., ed. *Library Orientation*. Papers presented at First Annual Conference on Library Orientation, Ypsilanti, Mich., Eastern Michigan Univ., May 7, 1971. Ann Arbor, Mich.: Pierian Pr., 1972. Available from ERIC no. ED 063 004.

Marchese, Theodore J. "Toward a More Effective Experience for Freshmen." Paper presented at CASC Workshop, Spring Arbor, Mich., Aug. 10, 1972. Available from ERIC, no. ED 065 106.

Massachusetts Univ. School of Education. *Survey Report of State-funded College Programs for "Disadvantaged" Students in Massachusetts*. Amherst: Massachusetts Univ. School of Education, 1972. Available from ERIC, no. ED 063 836.

Menzel, Dennis. "Theoretical Issues Involved in Educating the Disadvantaged" (1969). Available from ERIC, no. ED 039 833.

Monlouis, Wilma D. "Higher Education Opportunities for High-Risk Disadvantaged Students: A Review of the Literature." Washington, D.C.: ERIC Clearing House on Higher Education, Feb. 1970. Available from ERIC, no. ED 035 373.

Nyquist, Ewald B. "Education's Financial Dilemma: Planning for Change or Reacting to Crisis." Speech given at sixth meeting of Education Commission of the States, Los Angeles, May 17, 1972. Available from ERIC, no. ED 064 770.

Olsen, Henry D. "Changes in Academic Roles of Black and White Compensatory Education Students and Its [sic] Effects on Self-Concept-of-Academic Ability." Paper presented at Annual Meeting of American Educational Research Association, Chicago, Apr. 3–7, 1972. Available from ERIC, no. ED 063 219.

"The Open Admissions Story: 1970 at the City University of New York." New York: City Univ. of New York Office of University Relations, Dec. 3, 1970. Available from ERIC, no. ED 048 820.

Ravetch, Herbert. "Individualization of Instruction: The Junior College Takes a Page from the Elementary-Secondary Notebook." Los Angeles: Univ. of California, 1968. Available from ERIC, no. ED 031 211.

Rosener, Benjamin. "Open Admissions at the City University of New York." Paper presented at Annual Meeting of American Association of the Advancement of Science, Chicago, Dec. 27, 1970. Washington, D.C.: American

Association of the Advancement of Science, 1971. Available from ERIC, no. ED 050 676.

Trent, William T. "College Compensatory Programs for Disadvantaged Students" (1970). Available from ERIC, no. ED 042 394.

Wahlberg, William Auman. *The Effect of Process Intervention on the Attitudes and Learning in a College Freshman Composition Class.* Ann Arbor: Univ. of Michigan, 1970. Available from ERIC, no. ED 057 040.

Young, Arthur P.; Boone, Morell; and Salverson, Carol. "Survey of User Education in New York State Academic Libraries." Paper presented at New York Library Association Annual Conference, New York, Oct. 6, 1971. Available from ERIC, no. ED 055 621.

Conference Papers

Boone, Morell D.; Chapman, Edward A.; Mitchell, Basil; Overfield, Peggy A.; Salverson, Carol A.; Stein, Irwin S.; Young, Arthur P.; Lubans, John, Jr. *Use, Mis-Use and Non-Use of Academic Libraries: Proceedings of the New York Library Association—College and University Libraries Section.* Watertown, N.Y., May 1–2, 1970.

City University of New York. *Proceedings of the City University of New York Conference on Open Admissions.* New York, 1971.

Karkhanis, Sharad, and Sellen, Betty-Carol, eds. *A New College Student: The Challenge to City University Libraries.* Papers presented at Library Association of the City University of New York Institute, New York, Apr. 10, 1969. Rockaway Park, N.Y.: Scientific Book Service, 1969.

Schuman, Patricia, and Sellen, Betty-Carol, eds. *Libraries for the 70's.* Papers presented at Library Association of the City University of New York Institute, Apr. 2, 1970. New York: Queens College, 1970.

Unpublished Materials

Breivik, Patricia Senn. "The City University of New York Libraries and Open Enrollment." Columbia Univ. School of Library Services, 1971.

Brooklyn College. Department of Educational Services. "Department of Educational Services Handbook." New York, Brooklyn College, 1972, (mimeographed).

Brooklyn College Library. "Report of the Open Admissions Committee." Brooklyn College, Mar. 9, 1970.

————. Committee on the Master Plan. "Response to Questions in the 1972 University Master Plan Outline." Brooklyn College, July 23, 1971.

Colston, James A. "Open Admissions at City University." Speech given at Annual Spring Meeting of Beta Phi Mu, International Library Science Honorary Society, Theta Chapter, New York, May 2, 1972.

Lubans, John, Jr. "Study of the Library Use Habits and Attitudes of 'Academic Opportunity Students.'" Univ. of Colorado Libraries, 1970.

Wright, Sylvia Hart. "Backing Up a Remedial, Pre-College Program." New York, City College, 1965.